Book Of Tale
Sippurei Maasiyot

Rebbi
Nachman of Breslov
13 stories

לְרַבֵּנוּ הַגָּדוֹל

נַחַל נוֹבֵעַ מְקוֹר חָכְמָה

רַבִּי נַחְמָן מִבְּרֶסְלָב

מוֹהֲרַ"ן

זצוקלה"ה

נין לרבינו הבעל שם טוב הקדוש

SimchatChaim.com

There is no known book without mistakes. Therefore, I ask in every language of application if anyone has any questions, comments, clarifications, corrections, please send to: simchatchaim@yahoo.com

All material used in this section may not be used for commercial purposes, but only for study and teaching.

To get this book or books and information Email me at:

simchatchaim@yahoo.com

Copyright©All Rights Reserved to

www.simchatchaim.com

Itzhak Hoki Aboudi ©All rights reserved to the Editor

Second edition 2024

Sippurei Maasiyot – Content of the book

Tales of Rebbi Nachman's of Breslov.

Content of the book

Page	Content
3.	Chapter 1 - The Princess Is Lost.
12.	Chapter 2 - The Emperor and the King.
28.	Chapter 3 - The Son Who Could Not Walk
45.	Chapter 4 - The King Who Decreed.
53.	Chapter 5 - The King's Son Who Was Made of Gemstones.
57.	Chapter 6 - The Humble King.
62.	Chapter 7 - The Fly and the Spider.
70.	Chapter 8 - The Rebbi and His Only Son.
75.	Chapter 9 - Wise and Innocent.
103.	Chapter 10 - The Burgher and the Pauper.
140.	Chapter 11 - The King's Son and Bondmaid's Son Who Were Switched.
170.	Chapter 12 - The Prayer Meister.
231.	Chapter 13 - The Seven Beggars.

Tales from ancient times are a collection of folktales in the style of folk tales that Rebbi Nachman of Breslov told to his students. His prominent student Rebbi **Natan** of Breslov recorded and published them. It is customary to think that there is a gothic and Kabbalistic dimension to these stories, and they differ in style and essence from the rest of the parables and stories told by Rebbi Nachman, which appear in his writings and the writings of his disciples.

One should know that these stories have deep secrets, blessed is he who gets to understand them.

Sippurei Maasiyot – Content of the book

Rebbi Nachman paved new ways in Chassidot. He emphasized the value of prayer, solitude, innocence and simple faith. Rebbi Nacham taught avoidance of philosophical inquiry, even though at the end of his life he befriended the educated Jews who lived in the city of **Uman**. He also stressed the need to long for God and said that according to his greatness there is no one who can say that he worships God, but the main thing is longing and longing. This longing can be gained mainly with the help of simple faith.

Along with the sermons he delivered to his followers, as was the custom of the rebbes of his generation, he also told tales, which are interpreted as allegories and complement his teachings.

He emphasized the importance of being joyful, and to the resist being despaired or sadness. This characterized throughout his teachings. Examples of his own famous sayings on this subject:

Know that man has to cross a very, very narrow bridge, and the rule is that you will not be afraid at all.

It is a great mitzvah to always be happy.

There is no despair in the world at all.

Sippurei Maasiyot – Chapter 1

Chapter 1

The Princess Is Lost

He answered and said, By the way I have told a deed, that every one that hath heard it shall have remembrance. And this is it.

And this is the story. The king had six sons and one daughter. The daughter was very dear to him, and he would cherish in other words, love her exceedingly and play with her very much. One time, while he was together with her on a certain day, he became angry with her and the words, "Let the Not-Good take you away!" escaped from his mouth. At night she went to her room; in the morning no one knew where she was. Her father (the king) was very afflicted and went here and there looking for her.

The second in kingship arose because he saw the king was very distressed, and asked to be given an attendant, a horse and money for expenses, and he went to search for her. He searched hard for her, for a very long time, until he found her. [Now he tells how he searched for her until he found her.]

He went a long time, in deserts, fields and forests, and was seeking her quite a long time. He was going around in desert area and saw a way from the side. He decided, "Since I have been going for such a long time in the

Sippurei Maasiyot – Chapter 1

wilderness and cannot find her, I will follow this path; maybe I will reach a settled area." He went for a long time.

Later on, he saw a castle and many soldiers standing around it. The castle was very beautiful, with the soldiers standing around it in fine order. He was afraid of the soldiers lest they not let him enter. He decided, "I will go and try," and he left the horse and went to the castle. They let him enter, and did not hinder him at all, so he went from room to room, and they did not stop him. He came to a palace and saw the king sitting there with a crown and many soldiers standing around him. And many were playing on instruments for him and it was very pleasant and beautiful there. And neither the king nor any of them asked the second in kingship a thing. And he saw their delicacies and good foods, and he went and ate, and went and lay down in a corner to see what would be done there.

He saw that the king called for the queen to be brought, and they went to bring her. And there was a great commotion and a great celebration, and the musicians played and sang vigorously because they were bringing the queen. And they placed a throne for her and seated her next to him. And she was the king's daughter, and he the second in kingship, saw her and recognized her. Later, the queen glanced and saw someone lying in a corner. She recognized him and rose from her throne, went to him, touched him and asked him, "Do you recognize

Sippurei Maasiyot – Chapter 1

me?" And he answered her, "Yes, I know you. You are the king's daughter who was lost."

He asked her, "How is it that you have come here?" She answered him: because that utterance slipped out from her father namely, that "the Not-Good should take you", and here, this is the place that is Not-Good." He told her that her father was very distressed, and that he had been searching for many years. And he asked her, "How can I take you out?" She answered him, "You cannot take me out unless you choose for yourself a place and remain there for one year; and the entire year you must yearn for me, to take me out; and whenever you have free time you must only yearn, ask and hope expectantly to take me out, and you must fast. And on the last day of the year, you must fast and you must not sleep the entire 24 hours period." He went and did so, and at the end of the year on the last day he fasted and did not sleep, and he arose and went there that is, to the king's daughter, to take her out. He beheld a tree; on this tree grew very beautiful apples. He had a big craving for it and he went and ate from them. As soon as he ate the apple, he fell down and sleep overtook him, and he slept a very long time. His attendant tried to wake him, but he could not be awakened at all.

Later he awoke from his sleep and asked the attendant, "Where am I in the world?" He the attendant told him the whole story. "You have been sleeping a very long time. It is already

Sippurei Maasiyot – Chapter 1

several years. And I have sustained myself from the fruit." He the-second in kingship agonized very much, and went there and found her there that is, the king's daughter. She lamented to him very much. "If you would have just come on that day you would have taken me out of here, and because of one day you lost. In other words, because you could not restrain yourself one day and you ate the apple, because of that you lost. In truth, not to eat is a very difficult thing, especially on the last day, when the evil inclination becomes very strong. [That is, the king's daughter said to him that now she would make the prohibition more lenient, and he would not be forbidden to eat, because it is a hard thing to abide by, etc.] Therefore, choose for yourself a place again, and also stays there a year, as before, and on the last day you will be permitted to eat only, do not sleep, and do not drink wine so that you will not sleep, because the main thing is sleep." He went and did so.

On the last day he was going there, and he saw a running spring, and its color was red and the smell was of wine. He asked the servant, "Have you seen? This is a spring, and there ought to be water in it, but its color is red and the smell is of wine!" And he went and tasted from the spring. He immediately fell down and slept many years, until seventy years. There were many troops going along, with their trains that follow behind them, and the servant hid himself because of the soldiers. After that went

Sippurei Maasiyot – Chapter 1

a carriage and covered wagons, and there sat the king's daughter. She stood next to him, went down and sat next to him and recognized him. And she tried very much to wake him, but he could not be woken. She started to lament over him, that "so many, so many great efforts and toils you tortuously made these many, many years in order to take me out, and for one day, when you could have taken me out, you completely lost," and she cried very much about this. She said, "It is a great pity on you and on me, that I am here such a long time and cannot go out," etc. Afterwards she took the scarf off her head, and wrote on it with her tears and laid it down next to him, and stood up and sat in her carriage and rode away.

Afterwards he awoke and asked the attendant, "Where am I in the world?" He told him the whole story, and that many troops passed through there, and that the carriage was here, and that she [the king's daughter] screamed, "It is a great pity on you and on me" etc. as before. Meanwhile, he glanced and noticed the scarf lying next to him. He asked, "Who is this from?" He answered him, "She left it behind and wrote on it with her tears." He took the scarf and raised it up against the sun and began to see the letters. He read what was written there: her lamentation and her cries, as mentioned; and it was written there that now, she is no longer in the castle; he should just search for a golden mountain and a pearl castle; "There, you will find me." He left the attendant behind and went alone to seek her. And he went and sought her for many years. He decided that in a settled area there cannot be a golden mountain and a pearl castle, because he was an expert in the world map. "Therefore, I will go in the deserts." He went searching for her in deserts for many years.

Afterwards he noticed a very large man whose largeness was beyond human bounds and he was carrying a large tree, so large that in a settled area such a large tree would not exist, and he giant asked him, "Who are you?" He answered him, "I am a man." He was amazed and said, "I have been in the wilderness such a long time now, and I have never seen a man." He told him the whole story mentioned above and that he's looking for a golden mountain and a pearl castle. He replied to him, "It certainly does not exist." And he dissuaded him and said to him, "They have convinced you with nonsense, because it certainly does not exist." He started to weep very much the second in kingship cried very much and said, "With certainty it does exist, in some place." But he dissuaded him and said, "Certainly they have convinced you with nonsense." He said, "Certainly it exists somewhere!" He said to him, "In my opinion it is nonsense, but because you are so stubborn, look I am the appointee over all the animals. I will act for your sake and summon all the animals. Since they run all over the world, maybe one of them will know of that mountain and that castle." He summoned all

Sippurei Maasiyot – Chapter 1

the animals from small to large, all sorts of animals, and asked them. They all replied that they had not seen. He said to him, "See, they have talked nonsense into you. If you want to listen to me, turn back, because certainly you will not find it, because it does not exist in the world." But he pressed him very much and said, "It must surely indeed be!" He said to him, "Look, I have a brother in the wilderness and he is the appointee over all the birds. Maybe they will know, since they fly high in the air. Maybe they have seen this mountain and the castle. Go to him, and tell him that I've sent you to him."

He went many, many years seeking him the appointee over the animals and again found a very large man, as before, and he also carried a large tree and also questioned him as before. He answered him with the whole story and that his brother had sent him to him, and he too dissuaded him the second in kingship since, "This certainly does not exist;" and the second in kingship also disputed with him, "It certainly does exist!" He told him this man told the second in kingship, "I am the appointee over all the birds; I will summon them; maybe they will know." He called up all the birds and asked all of them, from small to large. They answered him that they do not know of the mountain and the castle. He told him, "Don't you see it is certainly not here in the world? If you will listen to me, turn back, because it certainly is not here." And he pressed him and said, "It

Sippurei Maasiyot – Chapter 1

certainly is here in the world!" He told him, "Further in the wilderness is my brother; he is appointee over all the winds and they run over the whole world; perhaps they know."

He went many, many years seeking him and again found a large man, as before, who was also carrying a large tree and also questioned him, as before. He also answered him with the whole story, as before. He also dissuaded him, and the second in kingship implored him likewise. He said to him this third man to the second in kingship that he would act for his sake and summon the winds and ask them. He called them and all the winds came and he asked all of them. Not one of them knew of the mountain and the castle. He said to him, the third man to the second in kingship, "Don't you see that you have been told nonsense?" The second in kingship began to cry very much and said, "I know it surely does exist!"

He went many, many years seeking him and again found a large man, as before, who was also carrying a large tree and also questioned him, as before. He also answered him with the whole story, as before. He also dissuaded him, and the second in kingship implored him likewise. He said to him this third man to the second in kingship that he would act for his sake and summon the winds and ask them. He called them and all the winds came and he asked all of them. Not one of them knew of the mountain and the castle. He said to him, the third man to the second in kingship, "Don't you

Sippurei Maasiyot – Chapter 1

see that you have been told nonsense?" The second in kingship began to cry very much and said, "I know it surely does exist!"

The appointee over the winds replied to the second in kingship, "Since it is such a long time that you have been searching for her, and you have spent so much effort, and perhaps you will now have a hindrance due to money, therefore I will give you a vessel, such that when you put your hand into it, you will get money from there." And he summoned the wind to carry him there. The storm wind came and carried him there and brought him to the gate, and standing there were soldiers who did not let him enter the city. He put his hand into the vessel and took out money and bribed them and went into the city. It was a beautiful city. And he went to a man of means and rented food and lodging for himself, for one must remain there, for one needs to see with wisdom and intellect in order to take her out. And how he took her out, he did not tell. But in the end, he took her out.

Chapter 2

The Emperor and the King

Once there was an emperor. The emperor had no children. And there was also one king; the king also had no children. The emperor let himself wander the earth searching: perhaps he would find some solution or treatment so that he would have children. The king also let himself travel the world. The two of them came together at one inn and they did not recognize each other. The emperor recognized in the king that he had royal mannerisms and he asked him, and he acknowledged to him that he was a king. The king also recognized in the emperor that he had royal customs, and he also acknowledged it to him. They told each other that they were traveling for children. They enacted between them that if they would come home and their wives would bear one a boy and one a girl, they would match them. The emperor traveled home and had a daughter and the king traveled home and had a son - and the match was forgotten by them. The emperor sent his daughter to study. The king also sent his son to study. They both arrived at the same teacher; they liked each other very much. They agreed between themselves to marry each other. The prince took a ring and placed it on her hand; they were espoused.

Sippurei Maasiyot – Chapter 2

Afterwards, the emperor sent for his daughter and brought her home. The king also sent for his son and also brought him home. Matches were suggested for the emperor's daughter, but she was not interested in any match on account of the bond she had already made with the king's son. The king's son yearned for her greatly, and the emperor's daughter was also constantly sad. The emperor would walk her through his courtyards and palace, showing her greatness, but she was always sad. The king's son yearned for her so much that he became ill, and no matter how much he was asked, "Why are you ill?" he did not want to say. They asked the one who served him, "Maybe you can clarify by him?" He answered them, "I know," because the one who served him was with him there where he learned. He told them that is, the servant told them why he was sick. The king remembered that he had already long ago made a match with the emperor, so he went and wrote to the emperor that he should prepare himself for the wedding, for the match had indeed been made long ago, as mentioned. And the emperor no longer wanted the match, but he could not brazenly refuse. The emperor wrote that the king should send his son to him, in order for him to see if he could rule countries; then he would give him his daughter. The king sent his son to him. The emperor sat him down in a room and gave him papers of government matters in order to see if he could lead a country. The king's son was deeply yearning to

Sippurei Maasiyot – Chapter 2

see her, but he could not see her.

Once time, while he was walking along a wall of mirror, he saw her and fainted. She came to him and roused him, and she told him that she does not want any other match because of the bond she already had with him. He said to her, "What can we do? Your father does not want it." She said, "Nevertheless;" she would save herself just for him. Then they took counsel: they would let themselves go by sea. So, they rented a ship and set out on the sea; they traveled on the sea. Afterwards they wanted to come ashore, and they came ashore. There was a forest there, and they went into it. The emperor's daughter took the ring and gave it to him, and she lay down to sleep. Afterwards, the king's son saw that she would soon get up, so he put the ring next to her. Then they went to the ship.

Meanwhile, she remembered that they had forgotten the ring there, so she sent him after the ring. He went there, but could not find the place. He went further and still could not find the ring. He went seeking the ring from one place to another place, until he got lost and was unable to return. She went looking for him and she too got lost. He was going along and getting further and further astray. Then he saw a path and he entered a settled area. He had nothing to do, so he became a servant. She too went and got lost. She decided she would sit by the sea. She went to the shore of the sea, and there were fruit trees there. She settled there, and during the day she would go along the sea; perhaps she would find some passersby. And she sustained herself on the fruit, and at night she would climb up a tree to be protected from wild beasts.

The day came to pass, when there was a big merchant a very big merchant who had commerce throughout the entire world. And he had an only son. And the merchant was now old. Once the son said to his father, "Being that you are already old and I am still very young and your trustees do not supervise me whatsoever, what will happen? You will die, and I will be left alone; I will not at all know what to do. So, give me a ship with wares so that I can set out to sea in order to be experienced in commerce." The father gave him a ship with wares, and he went to countries and sold the wares and purchased other wares and was very successful. While he was at sea, he noticed the trees where the emperor's daughter was dwelling. They thought that it was a settlement; they wanted to go there. When they came near, they saw that they were trees; they wanted to go back.

Meanwhile, the merchant's son looked in the sea and saw a tree there upon which was the appearance of a human being. He thought that perhaps he was misleading himself, so he told the other men who were there. They too looked and also saw the appearance of a human on the tree. They decided to draw near there. They sent a man with a small boat, and they looked

Sippurei Maasiyot – Chapter 2

in the sea in order to guide the scout so that he could hit the tree. The emissary went there and saw that sitting there was a human, and he told them. He himself [the merchant's son] went there and saw her sitting there that is, the emperor's daughter, and he told her to come down. She said to him that she does not want to enter the ship unless he promises that he will not touch her until he arrives home and marries her lawfully. He promised her, and she entered with him into the ship. He saw that she could play musical instruments and speak several languages, and he rejoiced that she chanced upon him.

Afterwards as they began drawing near his house, she said to him that the proper thing would be that he goes home and informs his father, relatives, and good friends, that since he is bringing such a precious woman, they should all come out to greet her, and after that he would know who she is. [Because previously she had also made a condition with him that he should not ask her who she is until after the wedding, at which time he would know who she is]. He agreed to this. Further she said to him, "The proper thing is also that you should inebriate all the mariners who operate the ship, to let them know that their merchant is getting wed with such a woman," and he accorded with her. So, he took very fine wine that he had on board the ship and gave it to them; they got very drunk, and he went home to inform his father and friends. And the sailors were drunk

Sippurei Maasiyot – Chapter 2

and went out from the ship and they fell and lay drunk.

While they were preparing themselves to go greet her with the entire family, she went and untied the ship from the shore, spread the sails and was away with the ship. And the entire family came to the ship and found nothing. The merchant was enraged at his son, and the son cried out, "Believe me! I brought a ship with wares!" etc. but they see nothing. He said to him, "Ask the sailors!" So, he went to ask them, but they lay drunk. Afterwards the sailors got up, and he asked them, but they knew nothing at all about what happened to them. They only knew that they had brought a ship with all the aforementioned, but they don't know where it is. The merchant was very angry at his son and banished the son from his home so that he should not appear before him. The son went away wandering about. And she that is, the emperor's daughter, was going on the sea.

The day came to pass when there was a king who had built himself a palace by the sea, for it pleased him there because of the sea air and because the ships go there. And the emperor's daughter was going on the sea and came near to this palace of the king. The king took a look and he saw the ship going without a crew and no one was there. He thought he was deceiving himself. He ordered his men to look, and they also saw. And she came closer to the palace. She decided: what does she need this palace for? and she started to turn around. The king

Sippurei Maasiyot – Chapter 2

sent and brought her back from her ship which she had turned around, and brought her into his home. Now, this king did not have any wife, because he could not choose for himself, because whoever he wanted did not want him and vice versa. When the emperor's daughter came to him, she told him to swear to her that he would not touch her until he legally marries her, and he swore to her. She told him that it would be right to not open her ship and to not touch it; to just let it stand like that in the sea until the wedding, in order that everyone would then see the vast wares she had brought, so that they should not say that he had taken a woman from the market. He promised her so.

So, the king wrote to all the countries to all come to the wedding. And he built a palace for her sake, and she commanded that they bring her eleven daughters of nobility to be with her. The king ordered, and they sent her eleven daughters of very high noblemen, and they built each one an individual palace, and she also had an individual palace. They would gather unto her; they would play musical instruments and play with her.

Once, she told them she would go with them on the sea. They went with her and were playing there. She told them she would honor them with good wine that she had. She gave them from the wine that was in the ship; they became drunk, fell down and remained lying. She went and unbound the ship, spread out the sails and fled with the ship. The king and his

Sippurei Maasiyot – Chapter 2

people took a look and saw that the ship was not there, and they were very panicked. The king said, "See to it that you do not tell her suddenly, for she would have great distress for, the king did not know that she herself had fled with the ship; he thought she was in her room, and she might think that the king had given the ship to someone. Rather, they should send her one of the young noblewomen to tell her tactfully. They went to one room and found no one. And likewise in another room they also did not find anybody, and so on in all eleven rooms they also found nobody. They decided the king and his people to send her an elderly noblewoman at night to tell her. They came to her room and also found nobody, and they were very terrified.

Meanwhile, the fathers of the young noblewomen saw they were not having letters from their daughters; they were sending letters and got no letters back. They personally got up and all went to them, and did not find any of their daughters. They were enraged and wanted to send the king to his death, for they were the royal ministers. However, they came to the decision, "What is the king guilty of that he should be sent to death? the king transgressed as a victim of circumstance." They agreed to remove him from kingship and drive him out. They deposed him and exiled him; he went on his way.

And the emperor's daughter who had fled was faring with the ship. Later, the young

Sippurei Maasiyot – Chapter 2

noblewomen awoke and began to play with her again as before, for they were not aware that the ship had already departed from the shore. Then they said to her, "Let's go back home!" She answered them, "Let's stay here a bit longer." Afterwards there arose a storm wind and they said, "Let's go back home!" She informed them that the ship had already long left from the shore. They asked her, "Why have you done this?" She told them she was afraid the ship might be wrecked because of the storm wind; therefore, she had to do so. They were faring on the sea, the emperor's daughter with the eleven noblewomen, and were playing musical instruments, and they came across a palace. The daughters of nobility said to her, "Let's approach the palace!" But she did not want to; she said that she also regretted having approached the previous palace of the king who wanted to marry her.

Later, they saw some kind of island in the sea, and they drew near there. There were twelve pirates there; the pirates wanted to kill them. She asked, "Who is the superior amongst you?" They showed her. She said to him, "What do you do?" He told her they were robbers. She said to him, "We too are robbers. Only, you rob with your might, and we rob with shrewdness, for we are learned in languages and play musical instruments. Therefore, what will you win if you kill us? Better to take us for wives and you will have great wealth too;" and she showed them what was on the ship for the ship

Sippurei Maasiyot – Chapter 2

belonged to the trader's son, with his great wealth. The pirates agreed to her words. The pirates also showed them their wealth, and brought them to all their places. And it was agreed between them that they should not marry them all at one time, but only one after the other; and a selection should be made to give each one such a noblewoman as befits him, according to his greatness.

Afterwards she told them that she would honor them with very good wine which she has on board the ship, which she does not use at all; only, the wine is kept in store by her until God brings her match. She gave them the wine in twelve goblets and said that all of them should drink to each twelve. They drank, got drunk and collapsed. She called out to the other noblewomen, "Go and each of you kill your man." They went and killed off all of them. And they found enormous wealth there, such as cannot be found with any king. They decided that they should not take any copper or silver, only gold and precious stones, and they threw out from their ship things which are not so important, and loaded up the entire ship with precious things, with the gold and precious stones that they found there. And they came to a decision to no longer go dressed as women, and they sewed men's clothing for themselves German style and went with the ship.

And the day came to pass, and there was an old king. The king had an only son, and he had made him a wedding and had transferred the

Sippurei Maasiyot – Chapter 2

kingdom to him. Once, he said to his father he would go on a leisurely trip with his wife on the sea so that she become accustomed to the sea air, lest at some time they would have to flee on the sea. The king's son went with his wife and with the royal ministers and set out on a ship, and they were very merry there and played freely. Later they said they would all take off their clothes; they did so, and nothing remained on them except their shirts. And they urged everybody who could, to climb up to the mast. The prince climbed up on the mast. Meanwhile, the emperor's daughter approached with her ship and saw this ship of the prince with the ministers. Initially, she was afraid of going there, then she came a bit closer; she saw that they were playing intensely, so she understood that they were not pirates. She began drawing closer.

The emperor's daughter announced to her retinue, "I can throw that bald-head guy down into the sea that is, the prince, who was climbing up the mast!" For the prince had a bald head. They said to her, "How is that possible? We are very far from them!" She answered them: she has a burning-lens, and with it she will cast him down. And she decided she would not knock him down until he reaches the very top of the mast, because as long as he was in the middle of the mast, were he to fall he would fall into the ship, whereas when he reaches the top then when he falls, he will fall into the sea. She waited until he was up on the

Sippurei Maasiyot – Chapter 2

top of the mast. She took the burning lens and held it facing his brain until it burned his brain. He fell down into the sea. When he fell down there was a great commotion there on the ship and they did not know what to do. How could they return home? For the king would die of heartbreak. They decided to go to the ship that they saw that is, to the ship of the emperor's daughter; perhaps there would be some doctor there on board who could give them a solution. They drew close to the ship and told them namely, the people who were on the emperor's daughter's ship that they should not have any fear whatsoever for they, the men of the king's ship would not do any thing at all to them, and they asked, "Maybe you have here a doctor who can advise us?" And they told the whole story and how the prince had fallen into the sea. **The** emperor's daughter instructed them to draw him out of the sea. They went and found him and took him out. The emperor's daughter took his pulse with her hand and said his brain had been burnt. They went and tore open his brain and saw it was as she had said, and they were awestruck that is, it was a great novelty to them how the doctor, that is, the emperor's daughter, had been so correct. And they requested that she go together with them to their home; she would be doctor to the king and would be very esteemed by him. She did not want to, and she said that she was not a doctor at all, only she knows such things. Now, the people of the prince's ship did not want to

Sippurei Maasiyot – Chapter 2

return home; the two ships went together. It pleased the royal ministers very much that their queen that is, the wife of the prince should take the doctor that is, the emperor's daughter who was going dressed as a male and they thought that it was a doctor: for they saw she was exceedingly wise, therefore they wanted their queen who was the wife of the prince who died to marry the doctor that is, the emperor's daughter and he would be their king. And their old king that is, the father of the king they would kill. Only, they were ashamed to tell the queen that she should marry a doctor. But the queen too was pleased to marry the doctor, only, she feared the country perhaps they would not want him to be king. They came to the decision to make balls that is, banquets so that while drinking, at a time of merriment, they would be able to talk about it. They made a ball for each one of them on a separate day.

When the day came for the ball of the **doctor** - that is the emperor's daughter, he gave them of his aforementioned wine that he had and they got drunk. When they were merry, the ministers said, "How beautiful it would be if the queen would marry the doctor!" The doctor - that is, the emperor's daughter, replied "It would surely be very beautiful! If only they said this with a not drunken mouth!" The queen also replied, "It would be very beautiful for me to marry the doctor! If only the country would agree to it!" The **doctor** repeated, "It would surely be very beautiful! If only they proposed

Sippurei Maasiyot – Chapter 2

this with not drunken mouth!" Afterwards, when they sobered up from their drunkenness, the ministers remembered what they had said and were embarrassed before the queen for having said such things. But they decided: the queen herself had also said it! And the queen too was embarrassed before them, but she decided: they themselves had also said it! Meanwhile, they began to talk about it, and so it was agreed; they betrothed - the queen with the doctor - that is, with the emperor's daughter whom they thought was a doctor, as mentioned and they went home to their country. When the country saw them coming, they rejoiced greatly, since it had been a long time since the prince was away with the ship. And they did not know where he was, and the old king had meanwhile died before they arrived. Meanwhile they noticed that their prince who was their king was not there. They that is, the country asked, "Where is our king?" They told them the whole story, that the prince had long been dead now, and that they had already taken a new king, who was accompanying them that is, the **doctor** who was emperor's daughter. The countrymen were very happy that they had received a new king.

The king that is, the emperor's daughter, ordered to announce in all countries that whosoever was present anywhere foreigner, guest, refugee or exiled should all come to his wedding. Not a single one should be absent. They would receive great gifts. And the king

Sippurei Maasiyot – Chapter 2

that is, the emperor's daughter also commanded to make fountains all around the city, so that anyone who wanted to drink would not have to go away to get a drink, but would be able to find a fountain next to him. And the king that is, the emperor's daughter also ordered for his picture to be drawn next to every fountain, and to station guards to watch for anyone coming along and looking hard at the picture that is, at the portrait of the king, who was the emperor's daughter, as mentioned and making a bad face, as someone who looks at something and is shocked or saddened; they should grab him and put him in prison. All this was done. And these three men came along that is, the first prince, who was the true groom of the emperor's daughter who had become king there, the merchant's son who had been banished by his father on account of the emperor's daughter who had fled from him with the ship and all its merchandise, and the deposed king also on account of her, who had fled from him with the eleven daughters of nobility, as mentioned. And each of the three recognized that this was her picture, and they gazed intensely and remembered and became very anguished. They were caught and placed in prison.

At the time of the wedding, the king that is, the emperor's daughter, commanded to bring the captives before him. The three were brought and she recognized them, but they did not recognize her, since she was dressed like a

Sippurei Maasiyot – Chapter 2

man. The emperor's daughter spoke up and said, "You, king that is, the exiled king, who was one of the prisoners, you were deposed on account of the eleven daughters of nobility who were lost. Take back your daughters of nobility. Return home to your country and to your kingdom." Because the eleven daughters of nobility were there with her here. "You, merchant that is, first she spoke to the deposed king; now she turned to speak to the merchant, that is, the merchant's son you were banished by your father on account of the ship with its merchandise that was lost from you. Take back your ship with all the merchandise. And for your money being out so long, you now have a much greater wealth on the ship, many, many fold more than there was before" for the same ship with all the merchandise belonging to the merchant's son, with which she had fled, was still with her in its entirety, and in addition to this was all the wealth which she had taken from the pirates, which was extraordinary wealth, many, many fold more. "And you, prince that is, the first prince who was truly her groom, come here and let's go home." They returned home. Amen and Amen.

Sippurei Maasiyot – Chapter 3

Chapter 3

The Son Who Could Not Walk

Once there was a sage. Before his death he called his sons and family and left them a will: that they should water fruit **Ilanoth** [trees]. "You may engage in other needs as well, but this you must constantly do: water trees." Afterwards the sage passed away and he left children. And he had one son who could not walk; he could stand, but he could not walk. His brothers would give him his needs for livelihood, and they gave him so much that he had leftover. He would save up for himself bit by bit whatever remained beyond his needs, until he had amassed a certain amount. He then came to the decision, "Why should I get a stipend from them? Better that I begin some commerce." And though he could not walk, he came up with the solution to hire a carriage, an **Ne'eman** [assistant] faithful or trusted one and a wagon-driver and to travel with them to Leipzig, and he would be able to conduct trade even though he could not walk. When the family heard this, it pleased them very much, and they also said, "Why should we give him subsistence? Better to let him make a livelihood." And they lent him more money so that he could conduct trade.

Thus, he did; he hired a carriage, an assistant and a wagon-driver, and he set out, and they

Sippurei Maasiyot – Chapter 3

came to an inn. The assistant said that they should spend the night there, but he did not want to. They pleaded with him, but he was stubborn with them. They traveled away from there and got lost in a forest and thieves ambushed them. And the thieves had come about according to a story: There was once a famine. Someone came to the city and proclaimed: Whoever wants food should come to him. Numerous people came to him. When he saw that the men who came to him were not useful to him, he would reject them. To one he would say, "You can be a craftsman," while to another he said, "You can be a miller." And he chose only intelligent youths, and went with them into the forest and proposed to them that they become thieves: "Being that from here there are roads to Leipzig, to **Breslau** [a city in Germany] and to other places, merchants travel through here. We will rob them. We will have money." So did the thief who had earlier made the proclamation in the city tell them. The thieves ambushed them that is, the one who could not walk and his men, namely the assistant and the wagon driver. The assistant and the wagon driver were able to flee and they fled; and he was left on the wagon. The thieves came to him and took from him the chest of money and asked him, "Why are you sitting?" He replied he could not walk. And they stole the chest and the horses, and he remained on the carriage.

The assistant on the wagon-driver, who had

fled away, came to the decision that inasmuch as they had taken out loans from feudal landlords, why should they return home where they could be placed in chains? Better to remain there where they had fled and be an assistant and wagon-driver there. Now, the one who could not walk, who remained on the wagon, as long as he had the dry bread that he had brought from home, he ate it. Then when it ran out and he had nothing to eat, he thought about what to do. He threw himself out of the carriage to eat grass. He slept alone in the field and was frightened and his strength was so taken from him that he could not even stand, only crawl, and he would eat the grass that was around him. And as long as he could reach grass and eat, he would eat there, and when the grass around him ran out so that he could no longer reach, he crawled further away and ate again. Thus, he ate grass for a time.

Once, he came to an herb the likes of which he had never eaten before. This herb pleased him very much, because he had been eating grasses for a long time, so he knew them very well, and such an herb he had never seen before. He came to the decision to tear it out with its root. Under the root was a diamond. The diamond was quadrangular, and each side had in it a different **Segulah** [a charm or special ability]. On one side of the diamond, it was written that whoever grasps that side, it would take him where day and night meet together, that is, where the sun and the moon gather in unison.

Sippurei Maasiyot – Chapter 3

When he tore out the herb with its root, which is where the diamond was it happened that he grasped that side, that is, the side which the **segulah** of it was it would take him to the place where day and night come together. It took him there, where day and night come together. He looked around and now he was there!

He heard the sun and the moon talking, and the sun was complaining before the moon, "Inasmuch as there is a tree that has many branches, fruits, and leaves, and each of its branches, fruits, and leaves has a **segulah** - one is conducive, to having children, another is conducive to livelihood, another is conducive to healing this sickness, another is conducive for another sickness; each tiny bit of the tree is conducive to something else - this tree should have been watered, and if it would be watered, it would be very specially potent. But not only do I not water it, I shine on it too and dry it out."

The sun responded, "That is what you worry about?! I will tell you a cure. Inasmuch as there is a path, and many paths branch off from that path: One is the path of the **tzaddikim** [righteous]. Even someone who is a tzaddik here, the dust from that path is sprinkled underneath each his steps, so that with each step he is stepping on that dust. Another is the path of heretics. Even someone who is a heretic here, the dust of this path is sprinkled underneath each of his steps, as mentioned. And there is the path of the insane. Even someone who is insane here, the dust of this

Sippurei Maasiyot – Chapter 3

path is sprinkled underneath each of his steps, as mentioned. And so, there are several paths. And there is a different path, being that there are tzaddikim who accept suffering upon themselves, the landlords march them in chains, and they have no strength in their feet: dust from this path is sprinkled underneath their feet so that they have strength in their feet. So go there, for there is plenty of dust there and you will have healing for your feet." All this did the sun say to the moon. And he heard all this. That is, the one who had no strength in his feet heard all this.

Meanwhile, he looked at the diamond on another side and saw that it was written there that whoever grasps that side, it would bring him to the path from which many paths go out namely, the path mentioned above, of which the sun informed the moon. He grasped that side and it carried him away to there that is, to the path. He placed his feet on the path whose dust was healing for the feet and he was immediately healed. He went and took the dust from all the paths and bound each dust separately in a bundle. Namely, he bound the dust from the path of the righteous separately, and likewise the dust of the remaining paths he bound separately; so, he made himself bundles from the powders and took them with him. And he came to a decision and went to the forest where he was robbed. When he arrived there, he chose a tall tree near the path from which the thieves go out to rob. And he took the dust of

Sippurei Maasiyot – Chapter 3

the righteous and the dust of the insane and mixed them together, and spread them on the path. And he went up the tree and sat there to see what would happen with them.

He saw the robbers going out, having been sent out by the elder robber mentioned above to rob. When the robbers came to that path, as soon as they took a step on the powder, they became tzaddikim and began to cry out for their years and days for having robbed until then and having killed numerous souls. But since it was mixed there with the powder of the insane, they became insane tzaddikim and began to argue with each other. One said, "Because of you we killed," and another said, "Because of you!" So did they argue until they killed each other. The elder robber sent more robbers, and it was also as before and they also killed each other. And so, it was each time until they were all killed off, until he namely the one who previously had no strength in his feet, who was up in a tree understood that there were none remaining of the robbers except for him alone namely the elder robber who commanded them all and one other. He went down from the tree and swept up the dust from the path, and sprinkled only dust from the path of the righteous, and went to sit in the tree again.

Now, the elder robber was very puzzled that he had sent all the thieves and none of them had returned. He decided to go personally with the one that still remained with him. And as soon as he came onto the path where the son

Sippurei Maasiyot – Chapter 3

mentioned above had sprinkled the dust of the righteous by itself, he became a **tzaddik**. He began to cry out to the other bandit over his soul, over how he had murdered so many souls and robbed so much. And he tore graves and was penitent and very remorseful. When he the son who was sitting in the tree saw he had remorse and was very penitent, he came down from the tree. As soon as the robber noticed a person he began to cry out, "Woe to me! I have done this and that! Woe! Give me penance!" He answered him, "Return to me the chest that you robbed from me." For, it was written by them on all the stolen goods, when it was stolen and from whom. He said to him, "I will immediately return it to you! I will even give you the troves of stolen goods that I have! Just give me penance!" He said to him, "Your penance is just to go into the town, call out and confess, I am the one who made the proclamation at that time - during the famine, that whoever wants food should come to me. And made many robbers, and I murdered and robbed many souls. That is your penance." The robber gave him all his troves, and went with him into the city and did so. Judgment was passed in that town that since he had murdered so many souls, he should be hanged, so people would know: meaning, so that others would be edified.

After this he that is, the one who previously had no strength in his feet, decided to go to the two thousand mountains mentioned above to

Sippurei Maasiyot – Chapter 3

see what takes place there. When he arrived there, he stood far from the two thousand mountains, and he saw there were many, many millions and billions of demon families, for they are fruitful and they multiply and they have children as do humans, so they are very numerous. And he saw their kingship sitting on a throne, upon which no one born of a woman meaning, no human had ever sat on such a throne. And he saw how they make scoffery: one tells over that he had harmed someone's baby; another tells how he had harmed someone's hand; another tells how he had harmed someone's foot, and other such scoffery.

Meanwhile, he noticed a father and mother walking and crying. They were asked, "Why are you weeping?" They answered: They have a son, whose routine was he would go his way and would return at the same time, but now it has been a long time and he still has not come. They were brought before the king. The king ordered to send messengers throughout the world to find him. As they were returning from the king, the parents met up with someone who used to go together with their son. He asked them, "Why are you weeping?" They told him. He answered them, "I will tell you. Being that we had a little island at sea, which was our territory the king to whom this island pertained went and wanted to build palaces there and had already laid a foundation. Your son said to me that we should harm him. We went and took

Sippurei Maasiyot – Chapter 3

away the king's strength. He got involved with doctors but they could not help him so he started getting involved with sorcerers. There was one sorcerer there who knew his family. He did not know my family, therefore he could not do anything to me but he knew his family, so he seized him and is torturing him severely." They brought him that is, the demon who was telling all this to the king and he told it over before the king too. The king said: "Let them return the strength to the king [to whom the island pertained]!" He replied, "There was someone by us who had no strength and we have given away the strength to him." The king said, "Let them take that strength away from him and return it to the king!" They answered him: He has become a cloud that is, the demon to whom they have given away the king's strength has become a cloud. The king said that they should, "Summon the cloud and bring it here." They sent an emissary for him.

He namely, the one who previously had no strength in his feet, who has witnessed all this decided, "I will go ahead and see how these people [these demons] become a cloud." He followed the emissary and came to the city where the cloud was. He asked the townspeople, "Why is it such a cloud here in town?" They answered him, "Here in town it is just the opposite; never a cloud here. Only for while has such a cloud enveloped the city." And the emissary came and summoned the cloud; it went away from there. He that is, the one who previously had no strength in his feet decided to follow them to hear what they were saying. He heard the messenger ask him, "How did it come to be, that you became a cloud here?" He answered him, "I'll tell you a story.

Once, there was a **sage**. And the emperor of the country was a big heretic, and he made the entire country into heretics. The sage went and summoned his whole family and said to them, 'Surely you see that the emperor is a big heretic and has made the entire country into heretics, and some of our family he has already made into heretics. Therefore, let us set out for the wilderness so that we will be able to remain in our faith in God, blessed be He. They agreed on this. The sage uttered a Divine Name; it brought them to a wilderness. This wilderness did not please him. He again uttered a Name; it took them to yet another wilderness. This wilderness too did not please him. He uttered another name; again, it took him to another wilderness. This wilderness did please him. And the wilderness was close to the two thousand mountains, mentioned above. The sage went and made a circle around them so that no one would be able to come near them.

"**Now**, there is a tree which if it would be watered, there would not remain any of us that is, of the demons. Therefore, some of us stand digging day and night, allowing no water to reach the tree." The other one asked, "Why do they have to stand day and night digging? Once they have dug one time then the water will be unable to come; it should suffice." He answered him, "Since there are gossipers among us, and these gossipers go and instigate disputes between the one king and the other king, and this causes wars, and the wars cause earthquakes, and the earth around the ditches falls in, which allows water to reach the tree; therefore, they must constantly stand and dig. And when there is a new king among us, they make all the mockery before him and they rejoice. One jests in how he harmed a baby and how the mother mourns over it, another shows another mockery, and similarly many various mockeries. And when the king gets into festivity he goes and takes a walk with his ministers and tries to uproot the tree. Because if this tree would not exist at all, it would be very good for us. And the king fortifies his heart exceedingly in order to uproot the tree entirely. When he approaches the tree, the tree gives a great shout, so a great fear falls on him and he must turn around.

"**Once**, a new king was appointed among us that is, among the demons, for all this did the cloud tell to the emissary, as mentioned. Great mockery was done before him, as mentioned, and he waxed quite joyous and made his heart very bold, and wanted to tear out the tree completely. So, he went out walking with his ministers, brazened his heart exceedingly, and ran to tear out the tree completely. When he arrived at the tree it let out a great cry at him, and a great fear fell on him; he turned around

Sippurei Maasiyot – Chapter 3

and was very angry. And he was coming back and meanwhile took a look and noticed men sitting this was the aforementioned sage with his men. The king sent from his people to do something that is, to harm them, as was their custom. When the sage's family saw them, they were overcome with fear. The elder that is, the sage called out to them. Do not fear. When the demons arrived there, they were unable to come close due to the circle that was around them. He sent other messengers but they too were unable to come close. The king came in great anger and went himself and he too was unable to come close to them.

"**He** asked the elder to let him in to them. The elder said to him, since you request it of me, I will indeed let you in, however it is not customary for a king to go alone, so I will let you in with one other. He opened a little door for them, they entered, and he closed the circle again. The king said to the elder, 'How do you come and settle on our place? He said to him, why is it your place? It is my place! The king said to the elder, you have no fear of me? He said, **No**. He said again, you have no fear at all? And he displayed himself becoming very big, up to the sky, and wanted to swallow him. The elder said, I still have no fear of you at all. But if I want, you will be afraid of me. And he went and prayed a bit, and big thick clouds formed, and there was great thunder. And thunder kills them very effectively, so all his ministers that were with him were killed, and none remained

Sippurei Maasiyot – Chapter 3

except for the king and the one who was there with him in the circle. He begged him that is, the king begged the elder for the thunder to cease, and it ceased.

"**The** king replied and said to the elder, 'Since you are such a person, I will give you a book of all the demon families. For, there are miracle workers who only know of one demon family, and even that family they do not know completely. But I will give you a book in which all the families are written. For, by the king they are all recorded, and even a newborn is also registered by the king. The king sent the one who was with him for the book. Hence the sage did very rightly by letting him in with another, for otherwise whom would he send? He brought him the book. He opened it and saw that inside were millions and billions of their families. The king promised the elder that they would never harm the elder's entire family, and he commanded to bring portraits of his whole family, and even if a baby was born, to immediately bring its portrait, so that they would not harm anyone from the elder's family.

Afterwards, when the time came for the elder to leave the world, he called his sons and commanded them and said to them, I leave you this book. Surely you see that I have the power to use this book in holiness, and even still I don't use it; I just have faith in Hashem Blessed. You too should not use it. Even if there will be one of you who will be able to use it in holiness, he still should not use it, but just

Sippurei Maasiyot – Chapter 3

have faith in Hashem Blessed. Then the sage died and the book was passed on as an inheritance and came to his grandson his son's son. And he had the power to use it in holiness, but he just had faith in Hashem Blessed, and did not use it, as the elder wished.

The gossipers that were among the demons tried to persuade the elder's grandson, since you have grown daughters and are unable to support them and marry them off, therefore use this book. And he did not know that they were trying to persuade him, and thought that his heart was advising him to do this. So, he traveled to his grandfather, to his grave, and asked him, being that you left a testament that we should not to use this book, but only have faith in Hashem Blessed, now my heart is telling me to use it. His grandfather who was deceased answered him, even though you can use it in holiness, it is better that you should have faith in the Hashem Blessed, and not use it, and Hashem Blessed, will help you. And that is what he did.

And the day came to pass, when the king of the country where this grandson of the elder lived became ill. He got involved with doctors, but they could not heal him. Due to the high heat there in that country, the treatments did not help. The king of the country decreed that the Jews should pray for him. Our king that is, the king of the demons said, since this grandson has the power to use this book in holiness and he still does not use it, therefore we need to do him a favor. He commanded me to become a cloud there so that the king of that country would be healed by the treatments that he had already taken and the treatments he would yet take. And the grandson knew nothing about this. And that is why I have become a cloud here." All this is what the cloud told the emissary.

And the one who previously had no strength in his feet was following them and heard everything. The one who was a cloud was brought before the demon king, and the king commanded to take the strength from him and return it to the other king from whom they had taken away his strength because he had built upon their territory, as mentioned, and they returned the strength to him. The son of the demons whose father and mother had wept for him, as mentioned had returned, and he arrived very afflicted and without strength, because he had been severely tortured there. He was very enraged at the sorcerer who had tortured him so much there, so he ordered his children and his family to always stalk this sorcerer. But among the demons are talkers that is, gossipers, and they went and told the sorcerer that they were waiting to ambush him, so that he could protect himself from them. The sorcerer performed some strategy, and called upon more sorcerers who knew more families, in order to protect himself from them. The demon son and his family were very enraged at the tattlers for having revealed his secret to the sorcerer.

Sippurei Maasiyot – Chapter 3

Once, it happened that some members of the demon son's family and some of the tattlers went together on the king's watch. The son's family went and made false accusations against the tattlers, and the king killed the tattlers. The remaining tattlers were enraged, and they went and made an upheaval that is, a huge war between all the kings. And there were hunger, infirmity, murder, and plagues among the demons. So, wars were waged between all the kings, and this caused an earthquake, and all the earth [around the tree] fell in, and the tree was watered completely. None of them that is, of the demons survived whatsoever, and they became as if they had never existed. Amen.

The secret of this story is alluded to in Chapter 1 in the Psalms of King David: - Fortunate is the man who has not walked..." the "path of the wicked" and the "path of the just." These are the aspect of the paths mentioned in the story that have the dust that they sprinkle, etc.... And he will be like a tree planted by streams of water, which gives its fruit in its season, and its leaves... and all that he does will prosper" this refers to the tree in the story, that all of its fruit and leaves, everything in its entirety, are all very beneficial, as mentioned.

Examine and you will find more allusions: "Fortunate is the man who has not walked" - "For, initially he could not walk. Has not stood" - For, later on, he could not stand either. And in the company of scorners" refers to the settlement of the mockers who make mockery,

Sippurei Maasiyot – Chapter 3

etc., as mentioned. Like chaff which the wind drives away" refers to the wind that carries away the dust. And all this is just a few superficial allusions that he [Rabbi Nachman] enlightened our eyes with a little bit, in order to somewhat understand and comprehend the extent to which these things reach. But the things are still sealed in utter concealment, for all these stories that he [Rabbi Nachman] told are very, very high above human comprehension and hidden from the eye of all living creatures, etc.

Chapter 4

The King Who Decreed

Once, there was a king who decreed religious exile over the country: that is, whoever wanted to remain in the country had to convert, otherwise be expelled from the country. There were some who abandoned all their goods and wealth, and they left in poverty, in order to remain in the faith and be able to be Jews. But some had pity on their wealth and remained there; they became **Anoosim** [compelled]: discreetly that is, in concealment, they practiced the religion of the Jews, but publicly that is, in front of people they were not allowed to conduct themselves as Jews.

Later the king died, and his son became king. And he began to rule the country very sharply that is, forcefully; heavy-handedly, and conquered many countries; and he was very wise. And because he held the royal ministers with a tight grip - very sharply in his hand, they banded together to attack him and kill him off with all his offspring.

And among the ministers was one of the **Anoosim**. He decided, "Why did I become an **Anoos**? Because I had pity on my possessions and my wealth. Now if the king will be killed and the country be left without a king, everyone will swallow his fellow alive, for a country cannot exist without a king." Therefore, he decided to go and inform the king, without them knowing. And he went and told the king that they had conspired against him, as mentioned. The king went and probed whether it was true, and he saw it was true, and he stationed guards. On the night they fell upon him they were caught and judged, each one according to his sentence.

The king spoke up and said to the minister who was an **Anoos** [forced convert], "What honor shall I give you for having saved me and my offspring? Shall I make you a minister that is, a Herr? You are already a minister! Give you money? You have money! Say what honor you want; I will surely do it for you." The **Anoos** answered, "But will you really do what I say?" The king said, "Yes, I will certainly do what you wish." The **Anoos** said, "Swear to me by your crown and your kingdom." The king swore to him. The **Anoos** replied, "My main honor is to be permitted to be a Jew in public to put on tallith and tefillin in public." The king was extremely disturbed, because in his entire country there were not allowed to be any Jews. But he had no choice because of the oath he had sworn, that whatever he wished he would do for him. In the morning the **Anoos** went and put on **Tallith and Tefillin** in public.

Later that king died and his son became king. The son began to rule gently, because he saw they had wanted to eliminate his father, as mentioned. And he conquered many countries and was extremely wise. The new king ordered

Sippurei Maasiyot – Chapter 4

a convening of all astrologers to tell him what sort of thing could cause his offspring to be cut off, so that he could guard against it. The astrologers told him that his offspring would not be cut off if he just guards himself from a bull and a ram that is, from an ox and a lamb; this was written down in the record book. The king ordered his children to also rule the country as he did, gently. Later he died.

His son became king, and he began to rule the country stringently, like his grandfather, and conquered many countries. And he fell upon a wisdom, and ordered to announce that no ox or sheep should be found in his country, so that his offspring could not be cut off. So, he thought he now had no fear of anything, and he ruled the country very stringently. And he became extremely clever. The king fell upon a wisdom that he could conquer the entire world without battle, for there are seven parts in the world, for the world consists of seven parts, and there are seven planets that is, seven luminaries that circle [that is, make a progression through] the seven days of the week and each planet shines on one of the seven parts of the world, and there are seven kinds of metals that is, seven different metals, namely gold, silver, copper, tin, etc. and each of the seven planets shines on a specific metal. The king went and gathered all the seven different metals and ordered to bring him all the golden portraits of all kings, which hang in their palaces, and he made a man from this. Its

Sippurei Maasiyot – Chapter 4

head was of gold, its body of silver, and likewise the rest of the limbs, of other metals; in this man were all seven kinds of metal. And he stationed the man on a high mountain, and all the seven planets shined in the man. And when a man needed any advice, or any commerce and did not know whether to do it or not, he would stand facing the limb of the type of metal pertaining to the part of the world where the man was from. And the man would contemplate whether to do the thing he needed or not. And if he needed to do it, that limb would light and shine and if not, it would darken. All this did the king do. And thereby he conquered the entire world and amassed a huge amount of money.

However, this effigy that he had made from the seven various metals was not able to perform unless the king cast down the haughty and raised the lowly that is, throw down big people from their greatness and pick up little people. He went and sent orders to all generals and other ministers who held positions of authority and orders merit badges and special privileges. They all came and he demoted them, removing their positions. Even those who had positions which they served since his great-grandfather he took them all away. And lowly people did he raise, appointing them to their places of the great people. Among the ministers whom the king was casting down was the **Anoos**. The king asked him, "What is your position?" He answered him, "My position is just to be

Sippurei Maasiyot – Chapter 4

permitted to be a Jew in public, for the favor that I did for your grandfather." The king took this from him, and he was again an **Anoos**. Once, the king lay down to sleep, and he saw in a dream the clear sky and he saw all **Twelve Mazaloth** [constellations] that is, the stars in the sky are partitioned into twelve parts, corresponding to the twelve months; a section of stars resembles a ram, which is the mazal of Nissan, and the mazal of Iyar is called **Bull**, that is, an **ox**; and so, each month has its mazal. And he saw the bull and the ram that is, the ox and the lamb that are among the mazaloth laughing at him. He awoke with great fury and was very frightened. He ordered to bring the chronicles that is, the book wherein everything is written down, and he saw it written there that by bull and ram his offspring would be cut off, and a great terror fell over him. And he told the queen, and a great terror also fell on her and her children. And his heart pounded hard and he called for all the dream interpreters. And each one interpreted individually, but nothing would enter in his ears. And an extremely great terror fell on him.

A sage came and told him that inasmuch as he had tradition from his father that the sun has three hundred sixty-five courses paths and there is a place upon which all the three hundred sixty-five of the sun's paths shine and an iron rod grows there, whoever has a fear, when he comes to the rod, will be saved from the fear.

Sippurei Maasiyot – Chapter 4

This pleased the king very much, and he went with his wife, children and all his descendants to that place, and the sage also went with them. But in the middle of the way stands an angel who is in charge over anger. For, by anger one creates a destructive angel that is, an angel that destroys and ruins, and this angel is appointed over all the destroyers. And he is asked the way, for there is a good path for a man, and there is a path full of mud, and there is a path full of pits, as well as other paths. And there is a path where there is fire that incinerates from **Four Miles** [parsa'oth is 3.7 kilometer] away. They asked the angel the way, and he told them the path where the fire is.

And the sage kept looking around to see if the fire was there, for he had a tradition from his father that the fire was there. Meanwhile he saw the fire, and he saw kings and Jews dressed in **Tallith and Tefillin** going around in the fire. only: This was because by those kings there lived Jews in their countries, therefore they were able to pass through the fire. The sage said to the king, "Since I have a tradition that **Four Miles** from the fire one is incinerated, I will go no further. You, if you wish, go." And the king thought that since he saw other kings walking around there in the fire, he would also be able to go there. The sage replied, "I have a tradition from my father, so I do not want to go. You, if you wish, go yourself." The king went with his entire offspring. They caught the fire and he and his entire offspring were incinerated and all

Sippurei Maasiyot – Chapter 4

cut off.

When the sage came home, it was a wonder to the ministers that the king and his offspring were cut off. Had he not guarded himself from a bull and a ram? How was it that his offspring and he were cut off? The **Anoos** replied, "Through me has he been cut off. For, the astrologers saw that by an ox and lamb his offspring would be cut off, but they did not know what they saw. For, an ox from its hide they make tefillin; and a lamb from its wool they make **Tzitzith for the Tallith**. And by them was the king and his offspring cut off. For, the kings where Jews did live in their countries, wrapped in tallith and tefillin, were able to go in the fire completely unharmed. But this king, because no Jews dressed in tallith and tefillin were allowed to dwell in his country, was therefore cut off, with his offspring. And this was the bull and the ram of the mazaloth laughing at him. For, the astrologers saw that by bull and ram would his offspring be cut off; they did not, however, know what they saw, and the king was cut off with his offspring." Amen, so let all Your enemies be obliterated, Hashem!

"**Why** are the nations in an uproar? ... You will break them with a rod of iron". the iron rods." ... lest He be angry and you perish in the way," etc. And the words are extremely archaic and closed up... All this I [Rabbi Nathan] heard.

In addition, I have found some more allusions from this story in this chapter: "... Let us break their bands asunder, and cast away their cords from us" bands are made of hide, the aspect of **Tefillin**. Avot are cords, aspect of **Tzitzith**, as our Rabbis Obm expounded this verse in tractate regarding **Tzitzith and Tefillin**. "He Who dwells on High will laugh" for, the bull and the ram laughed at him. "Then He speaks to them in His wrath; and He panics them with His sore displeasure" the anger, the panic and the tear mentioned above. "But I have poured/ anointed My **King on Tzion**. My holy mountain" perhaps the allusion here is to the effigy that the king erected on the high mountain; everything in holiness has its counterpart in evil, and this is counterpart to the king on the holy Mount Tzion, for, all the parts of the world are included there, and so forth, and this is the "mountain" there. **Nasakh** is a term as in "pouring and pouring-molding" the statue. All the advices mentioned above. "Nations as your inheritance, and the ends of the earth for your possession" to grasp together all ends of the earth, namely all seven parts of the world, and all the kings and nations as inheritance under him. Is Tefillin, and rejoice upon the trembling" the trembling. The entire story is hinted in this chapter, so well-off is he who will know something of these stories, which are great secrets of the Torah throughout.

Chapter 5

The King's Son Who Was Made of Gemstones

There was once a king who had no children. He went and got involved with doctors so that his kingdom should not be turned over to strangers, but they did not help him. So, he decreed on the Jews to pray for him to have children. The Jews sought a tzaddik to pray and because it happens that the king should have children. They sought and found a hidden tzaddik, and they told him to pray for the king to have children. He replied: he knows nothing at all [**Gar Nisht**]; they informed the king inasmuch as there was a hidden tzaddik there, but he said he knew **Gar Nisht**. The king sent a royal order for him, and they brought him before the king. The king began talking kindly with him, "You know very well that the Jews are in my hands. I can do with them what I will. Therefore, I ask you with goodness, pray that I have children." The tzaddik ensured the king that same year he would have a child, and he went home. The queen bore a daughter, and this queen's daughter was extremely beautiful. When she was four years old, she knew all the wisdoms and languages, and could play musical instruments. Kings from all countries would travel to see her, and it was a great joy for the king.

Sippurei Maasiyot – Chapter 5

Afterwards the king very much wanted to have a son so that his kingdom should not go away to a stranger, so he again decreed on the Jews that they should pray for him to have a son. They were searching for the first tzaddik, but they could not find him, for he had already passed away. They continued searching and they found another hidden tzaddik. And they told him that he should give the king a son, and he said that he does not know anything. Again, they informed the king, and the king said to the tzaddik also as before, "You know very well the Jews are in my hand, etc." The sage that is, this tzaddik said to him, "But will you be able to do what I order?" The king said, "Yes."

 The sage said to him, "I need you to bring all the types of **Gemstones** [lit. good stones], because each gemstone has in it a different **Segulah** [ability, charm]." And by the kings there is a book wherein are written all the types of gemstones. The king said, "I will spend half my kingdom in order to have a son." And the king went and brought him all the types of gemstones.

The sage took them and ground them, and took a goblet of wine and poured them in the wine. And he gave a half cup of wine to the king to drink, and the other half to the queen. And he told them that they would have a son who would be thoroughly of gemstones, and he would have in him all the **Seguloth** of all the gemstones, and he went home.

The queen gave birth to a son, and the king

Sippurei Maasiyot – Chapter 5

rejoiced very greatly, but the son that was born was not made of **Gemstones**. When the son was four years old, he was extremely handsome, very wise in all the wisdoms, and knew all the languages. Kings traveled to see him. Now, the princess saw that she was no longer so important, and she was jealous of him. The only consolation for her was that the tzaddik had said that he would be completely of gemstones; good that at least he was not made of gemstones. Once, the prince was carving wood and he nicked his finger. The princess ran to bandage his finger and she saw a gemstone there. She was extremely jealous of him, and she made herself sick. Many doctors came but were unable to heal her at all. Sorcerers were called. A sorcerer was there, to whom she disclosed the truth, that she had made herself sick because of her brother, as mentioned.

And she asked the sorcerer if it were possible to perform a spell on a man to become leprous. He said, "Yes." She said to the sorcerer, "What if he asks another sorcerer to annul the spell so that he will be healed?" The sorcerer said, "If the sorcery is thrown into the water, it can no longer be annulled." She did so and threw the sorcery into the water. The prince became very leprous. He had leprosy on his nose, on his face and on the rest of his body. The king got involved with doctors and with sorcerers, but they were of no avail. The king decreed on the Jews to pray. The Jews sought the Tzaddik -

who had prayed for the king to have a son, as mentioned, and brought him before the king.

Now, this Tzaddik would always pray before God blessed be He. Inasmuch as he had promised the king that his son would be completely made of **Gemstones**, and it had not been fulfilled. And he complained to the God blessed be He. - "Have I done this for honor's sake? I have done this only for Your honor, and now, it has not been fulfilled the way I said." And the Tzaddik came to the king. The Tzaddik had prayed namely, for the leprosy of the prince to be healed, but to no avail. He was informed that it was sorcery.

Now, this Tzaddik was higher than all sorcery. The Tzaddik came and informed the king that it was a sorcery, and that the sorcery had been thrown into the water, so the prince could not be healed except by throwing the sorcerer who performed the spell into the water. The king said, "I give you all the sorcerers to throw into the water so that my son be healed."

The princess was afraid, so she ran to the water to pull the sorcery out of the water, for she knew where it was. She fell into the water. A great tumult erupted over the princess falling into the water. The Tzaddik came and said that the prince would be healed. And he was healed, the leprosy withered up and fell off, and his entire skin peeled off. And he was entirely of gemstones, as the tzaddik had said.

Chapter 6

The Humble King

There was once a king who had a wise man. The king spoke up to the wise man, Inasmuch as there is a king whose signature declares that he is a great man of might, and a man of truth, and humble in other words, a truthful person who does not focus on himself [lit. hold of himself]: mighty - I know that he is a great man of might, for the sea flows around his country, and on the sea is stationed a navy on warships with cannons and they do not allow anyone to approach, and inwards from the sea there is a great swamp a place where one drowns surrounding the country, through which there is only one narrow path wide enough for only one person to pass; there too cannons are positioned, so that if someone comes to attack, the cannons are fired, so it is impossible to set foot there.

But his signing himself as being a man of truth and humble - this I do not know, and I want you to bring me this king's portrait. For the king had all the portraits of all the kings, but the portrait of that king who signs himself in such fashion as mentioned was not found by any king, for he is concealed from people, since he sits under a and he is far from his **Killah** [veil], countrymen.

The wise man went to that country. He came to

Sippurei Maasiyot – Chapter 6

the realization that he must come to know the essence of the country in other words, the "thing" of the country; how the country works. And how can he find out the country's essence? by way of the country's Jests. Because when one needs to know the essence of something, one must know its jesting. For there are many types of jesting: there is one who really wants to smite the other with his words, and when the other takes notice [lit. looks around] he says to him, "I am joshing! I drive a jest as in the verse - Like one who wearies himself shooting firebrands... and says, Am I not joking? and so there is someone who really means a jest but still harms the other with his words. Thus, there are several kinds of jesting.

Now, among all the countries, there is a country that includes all countries that is, the country is the principle and rule for all countries, and in that country, there is a city that includes all cities of that whole country that includes all the countries. And in the city is a house that includes all the houses of the entire city that embodies all cities of the country that includes all countries. And there in the house is a person who includes the entire house which includes etc. And there, there is someone who makes all the wisecracks and jesting of the entire country.

So, the wise man took a large amount of money with him and went there. He saw them making all types of fun and joking. He understood from the jests that the country is full of falsehood

Sippurei Maasiyot – Chapter 6

through and through. For he saw them making fun of how people are cheated in business, and how he goes to the **Ministrant** [lower court] and there it is utter lies and they take bribery there; and he goes to the **Sand** [higher court]. And there as well it is utter lies. And they were all making fun and jest, enacting all these things. The wise man understood from this jesting that the country is full of lies and deceit, lacking any truth in the land whatsoever. So, he went and did some commerce in the country and allowed himself to be cheated in the exchange, and went and brought suit before the **Sands**, they being all full of falsehood and bribes. On this day he gave them bribery; the next day they didn't recognize him. So, he went to a higher sand and there too it was full of falsehood. Until he came before the **Senate** [highest court] and there too it is falsehood and bribery throughout. Until he came to the king himself.

When he came to the king he spoke up and said, "Over whom are you king? The entire country is full of falsehood throughout, from beginning to end, and there is no truth in it here whatsoever." And he began to tell over all the falsehood of the country.

When the king heard his words, he bent his ear to the veil to listen to hear his words for it was a great wonder to the king that there should exist a man who would know all the falsehood of the country. And the royal ministers who heard the wise man's words grew very angry at

Sippurei Maasiyot – Chapter 6

him but he still continues reporting all the country's falsehood. The wise man spoke up, "One could say that the king is also like them; that he likes falsehood as the country does. But on the contrary one sees what a man of truth you are, and because of this you keep your distance from them: on account that you cannot bear the falsehood of the country." And he began to praise the king very very much.

And the king, because he was very humble - and in the place of his greatness, there is his humility, for that is the way of a humble man, that the more he is praised and extolled, the smaller to himself and the humbler he becomes - so on account of the wise man's great praise and exaltation of the king, the king entered into great humility and extreme tininess, until he became absolutely nothing; and he could no longer withhold himself and he threw aside the veil to see the wise man: who is it that knows and understands all this? The king's face was revealed, and the wise man saw him, depicted his portrait and brought it back to the king.

The paths of **Tziyon** are mournful. since the Temple has been destroyed, one is obligated to remember and mourn it, and unbridled joking and laughter are forbidden; **S'A'O'C'**. Also, there are no festivals or times when God can be **Seen**. **Tziyon** is the aspect of the **Tziyunim** [markers, placemarks] of all the countries, for they all gather there, as it is written. And see the bone of man, then shall he set up a sign by it. This is the meaning of, look upon **Tziyon**,

Sippurei Maasiyot – Chapter 6

the city of our assemblies, the acronym of which is **MeTzaCheiQ** [jesting], for that is where all the **Tziyunim** [signs] gathered, and whoever needed to know whether to do something or some business transaction would know it there. May it be His will that it be rebuilt speedily in our days, Amen.

Look, discern and gaze, reader, how far these matters reach. Fortunate is he who attends to and will attain knowing and grasping a little of the secrets of these stories, the likes of which have not been heard since ancient times.

And know, that all these verses and allusions that are brought after some of the stories are only hints and a scant disclosure of the subject matter, so that they might know - it is no empty thing, God forbid. As was heard from his holy mouth, saying that he is revealing a few mere hints from a few verses that hint to the secret of the stories, so as to know that he is not saying, God forbid, prattle. But the essential secret of the stories is far from our knowing; Deep-deep; who can find it out?"

Chapter 7

The Fly and the Spider

Rebbe Nachman announced, "I'll tell you my entire trip that I had." A tale. There was once a king who had a number of hard wars up against him, and he conquered them and took many captives. In the midst of his words as he began telling this story he interjected and said, "You might think mistakenly that I will tell you everything and that you will be able to understand." The king made a big banquet a ball every year on the day when he vanquished the war. There at the ball would be all the royal ministers and all the gentlewomen, as the usual way of kings goes, and comedy shows would be made and they would make fun of all the nations: of the **Ishmaelites** [Turk] and of all the nations. And they would imitate every nation in the way that their manner and conduct is, and they probably made fun of Jews as well.

The king ordered to bring the book in which the mannerisms and customs of every nation are recorded. And whenever the king would open up the book, he would see only: that written in it were the practices and mannerisms of the nation, exactly as they performed the parody of them, because probably the one who performed the comedy also saw the book. While the king was poring over the book, he saw a spider crawling on the edge of the book's

Sippurei Maasiyot – Chapter 7

pages, and on the pages stood a fly. Presumably, where does a spider go? - toward a fly. Meanwhile as the spider was crawling and going toward the fly, a wind came along and lifted that page from the book; the spider could no longer go to the fly. It turned around and crawled exactly as if it were turning around and no longer wants to go to the fly. Meanwhile, the page fell back in its place and again the spider wanted to go toward the fly. Again, the page lifted and did not permit it; again, the spider turned back. Thus, it happened several times. Afterwards again the spider went towards the fly and was crawling along until it had already gotten itself up with one foot on the page. Again, the page lifted up - and the spider was already somewhat on the page - then the page lay down completely, until the spider was left between one page and another; and it was crawling around there, but kept getting left deeper and deeper until nothing whatsoever was left of it. And the fly - I will not tell you what happened to it.

And the king had been watching all this and was very astonished; he understood that this is no empty thing but rather he is being shown something through it, and all the ministers saw that the king is gazing and wondering at it. And the king began thinking: what does this signify? And he dozed off over the book. The king dreamed that he was holding a diamond in his hand and looking at it. An exaggerated number of people were emerging from it and he threw the diamond down out of his hand. And the usual way by kings is that over them hangs their portrait and on top of the portrait hangs the crown. He saw in the dream how the people who had emerged from the diamond took the portrait and cut off its head, then they took the crown and threw it into the mud, and they ran towards him to kill him. A page from the book upon which he was lying lifted itself and shielded him and they were unable to do anything to him so they went away, then the page returned to its place. Then again, they wanted to kill him and again the page lifted itself as before. Thus, it happened several times. The king very much wanted to see what sort of page is shielding him that is, protecting him; what mannerisms are written on it; from which nation it is. But he was afraid to look and he began to scream, **Wwoe! Wwoe!** All the ministers who were sitting there heard and they wanted to wake him up; however, this is no sort of protocol, to wake up a king. They rapped around him in order to wake him, but he did not hear.

Meanwhile, a tall mountain came to him and asked him, "Why are you screaming so? It is such a long time already that I sleep and nobody at all has woken me up - and you have woken me up!" He said to him, "How shall I not scream, when they are rising up over me and want to kill me, except that this page is shielding me?!" The mountain answered him, "If this page is shielding you then you need have no fear of anything whatsoever, for many enemies rise against me as well, but this same page shields me. Come, I will show you." It showed him how around the mountain stand thousands and myriads of enemies and they make feasts and rejoice, playing musical instruments and dancing. And the joyful occasion is that some group from them, one of them thinks and arrives at some wisdom how to go up on the mountain, hence they make a big celebration and a feast with music and dancing, and thus with each group that is, faction from among them - "except that this page of these mannerisms that shields you shields me."

And on the mountain's peak is a tablet, and on it were written the mannerisms of the page that shields him; from which nations it is. But since the mountain is high, one cannot read the writing. However, at the bottom was a tablet; there it was written that whoever has all his teeth - he can go up on the mountain. God blessed be He provided that there grows such a grass there where one needs to go up on the mountain, that whoever comes there, all his teeth fall out; whether he was going by foot, riding, or driving a carriage by animals, always his teeth would fall out. Lying there were piles white with teeth, like mountains.

Later the people from the diamond took the portrait and put it back together as previously, and they took the crown and washed it up, and they hung them back in their place. And the

Sippurei Maasiyot – Chapter 7

king woke up and immediately looked at the page that had shielded him - which mannerism of which nation is it? He saw that written on it is the mannerisms of **Yisrael** [Jews]. He began to look at the page honestly and he understood the right truth, and he came to a decision that he himself would definitely be a **Yisrael** [Jew]. however, what does one do to return the entire world back to the best state, to bring them all to the truth? He came to the decision that he would journey in search of a sage who would solve the dream according to its essence that is, he should interpret the dream exactly as it is. And he took two men with him and traveled around the world, not as a king but as a simple person, and he traveled from one city to the next and he asked: where does one find such a sage who can solve his dream according to its essence? They informed him that there-and-there is found such a sage. He went there and came to the sage and told him the truth: that he is a king and he had vanquished wars, and the entire story that happened, as mentioned, and he asked him to solve his dream. The sage answered him, "I myself cannot interpret; however, there is a time on this day and in this month - then, I gather together all the spices of the Incense that is, all the herbs from which they would make the Incense and I make from them a compound in other words, he mixes them all up together and the person is smoked with the incense and this person thinks in himself what he wants to see and know, and

Sippurei Maasiyot – Chapter 7

then he knows everything."

The king resolved: since he has already in fact spent so much time on it, he would wait longer until that day and that month which the sage had told him. The day came and the sage did for him so, as described above, and smoked him with the incense. The king began to see even things that had happened to him before he was yet born, when the soul was still in the upper world in other words, on the other world; how they led his soul through all the worlds and they announced, "Whoever has something to say for the prosecution that is, to speak evil against this soul, let him come." There was no one who found fault. Meanwhile someone did come and was running and shouting, "Master of the World! Hear my prayer! If this one should come upon the earth, what then have I to do any longer, and for what have You created me? And this was the Samekh-Mem in other words, the one who was shouting was the **S.M** [Angel of Death] himself; he was yelling: if this soul should go down on the earth, he will no longer have anything to do. He was answered, "This soul must go down on the earth, and you - give yourself advice." He went away that is, the one who was yelling.

They led the soul further through worlds **Olamoth** [Spiritual worlds] a term for **World** whose root also denotes concealment; hence, the world as a clothing and concealment of the Blessed Unity in other words, worlds in order to swear it in already, in order that it should go

Sippurei Maasiyot – Chapter 7

down on the earth. And he had not yet arrived that is, the **S.M** [Angel of Death]. who was yelling earlier, had not come yet, so they sent an emissary after him? He came and brought with him a little oldster, a hunched-over one, with whom he was long familiar that is, the Accuser had been acquainted with this old one from long ago, and he laughed and said, "I have already given myself an advice; this soul can now go down on the earth." They released the soul and it went down on the earth. And he that is, the king saw everything that happened to him from beginning to end, how he became king, the wars he had, etc.

And he took captives, and among the captives was a beautiful woman who had every kind of charm in the world. However, this charm was not from herself; rather, she would hang a diamond upon herself and the diamond had all kinds of charm, and on account of that it seemed she had all kinds of charm. And upon that mountain can no others ascend except the wise, the rich, etc. And more than this he did not tell. And there is a great deal more in this. From "And he took captives" until the end - was not written properly as he told it.

A psalm of King David when he fled... Hashem, how many are mine adversaries become; many are they that rise up against me... But you, Hashem, are a shield about me: my glory and the lifter up of my head... With my voice I call out unto Hashem, and He answers me from His holy mountain, Selah -

Sippurei Maasiyot – Chapter 7

the mountain mentioned above. I lay down and I sleep - as mentioned above. I awake... I will not fear a multitude of people... for you have smitten all my enemies on the cheek; You have broken the teeth of the wicked - for their teeth would fall out when they wanted to go up on the mountain. May Your blessing be on Your people, Selah.

Stand and contemplate these wonders! If you are a living being **Baal Nefesh** [Possessed of a soul], take your flesh up in your teeth and place your Life **Nefesh** [soul] in your palm; stand trembling and amazed. Let the hairs of your head stand on edge, and return again and wonder at these words which stand in the highest of heights.

Chapter 8

The Rabbi and His Only Son

There was once a rabbi who had no children. Later, he had an only son and he raised him and made him a wedding. The son would sit in an attic room and learn and study Torah, as is the way with the wealthy. He would study and pray constantly, except that he felt in himself a lacking due to some deficiency, but he did not know what, and he had no taste satisfaction in his learning and praying. He told this to two young people and they advised he should travel to a certain **Tzaddik** [holy Jew]. Now, this son had done a certain **Mitzvah** [commandment in the Torah] through which he had reached the aspect of the Smaller Luminary. The only son went and told his father inasmuch as he feels no taste in his service meaning in what he serves God, namely praying, learning and other mitzvot, inasmuch that something is missing for him but he doesn't know what - therefore he wants to travel to this **Tzaddik** about whom they had told him, as above. His father answered him, "How do you come to decide he's worthy for you to travel to him? You are, after all, more scholarly and more pedigreed than he. It doesn't suit you to travel to him. Desist from this way!" Until the father thus dissuaded him from traveling to the **Tzaddik**. **The** son returned to his learning and again he

Sippurei Maasiyot – Chapter 8

felt the deficiency as mentioned above, and again he took counsel with those young people. Again, they gave him the advice that he should travel to the Tzaddik. Again, he went to his father and again his father diverted him and prevented him. This happened several times. And the son kept feeling his lack and he yearned to fill the void in other words, to correct something so he should not be devoid, but he did not know what was missing, as mentioned earlier. He went yet again to his father and begged him direly until his father felt compelled to travel with him. For his father did not want to let his son travel alone, since he was his only son. So, his father told him - Look, I will go with you. I'll show you that Tzaddik is nothing at all. They harnessed the carriage and set out. The father said to his son, "With this I will make a test: if everything goes orderly, it is from Heaven, and if not, it is not from Heaven that we should travel and we will return." They set out, and they reached a small bridge, a horse fell, the carriage turned over and they nearly drowned. His father said to him, "You see that it's not going orderly and the journey is not from Heaven." They returned. Again, the son returned to his studies and again he felt something lacking and he know not what. Again, he implored his father, as above, and his father had to once again travel with him. As they were traveling, his father again set up a test as before: if it goes orderly. As they were traveling, both axles broke. His father

Sippurei Maasiyot – Chapter 8

said to him, "See, events are not indicating we should travel. For is it a natural occurrence that both axles should break? How many times have we traveled with this carriage and such a thing has never happened?!" Again, they returned. And the son returned to his learning and so forth as above, and again he felt the deficiency as mentioned earlier, and the youths advised him to make the journey. Again, the only son went to his father and again pressed him; once again he had to travel with him. The only son told his father that "we should no longer set up such a test, for this is natural that sometimes a horse falls or axles can break - unless it will be something very shocking."

They traveled and came to an inn to spend the night. They met a merchant there, and they began talking with him as merchants are wont, not telling him that they are going there to one **Good Jew** [A Tzadik], for the rabbi was embarrassed to say that he's traveling to that tzaddik. They were speaking about worldly matters until the conversation came around the subject of tzaddikim; where tzaddikim are found. He the merchant told them in this certain place there is a tzaddik, and there and there. They began speaking about the tzaddik to whom they are traveling. The merchant answered them. That person in an expression of amazement? He is plainly a **light one**, in other words, not an earnest Jew! Just now I am traveling from him; I was there when he committed a transgression!" The father replied to his son, "Do you see, my son, what this merchant is telling us innocently? In other words, he is not intending trash-talk, to speak evil of the tzaddik; only by way of the conversation did he tell it. Look, he's coming right from there!" They returned home that is, the father and the only son.

The son died, and appeared in a dream to his father. His father saw him standing in great anger. His father asked him, "Why are you so angry?" The son answered that he should travel to that tzaddik to whom they had wanted to travel, "and he will tell you why I am angry." He awoke and thought to himself, "It's a coincidence." In other words, just a dream, not a truth. Then he again had the same dream, and again he thought, "It's a meaningless dream." When he dreamed it a third time, he understood that this is no empty thing and he traveled to that tzaddik. On the way he met the merchant whom he had previously encountered when traveling with his son. The rabbi recognized him and said, "Aren't you the one I saw at that inn?" He answers him, "Certainly you saw me!" The merchant opens up his mouth supernaturally wide and says to him, "If you want, I'll swallow you up!" The rabbi tells him, "What are you saying?!" He answered him, "Do you remember when you journeyed with your son, and the first time, a horse fell down on the bridge and you returned? Then the axles broke. Then you met me and I told you that he the Tzaddik is a a **light one**? Now that I have

Sippurei Maasiyot – Chapter 8

exterminated your son - now you may travel. For your son was an aspect of the Minor Luminary, and that tzaddik [whom he wanted to meet] is an aspect of the Major Luminary. If they would have assembled together, **Mashiach** would have come. And now that I have exterminated him, you are permitted to go." And as he was speaking, the merchant suddenly vanished. The rabbi didn't have with whom to talk, so he traveled to the Tzaddik and cried out, "Woe! Woe! Such a pity for that which is lost and unfindable!" May God blessed be He, return our exiled ones soon, Amen.

The merchant was the **S.M** [Angel of Death] himself, who disguised himself as a merchant and deceived them. Then when he met the rabbi the second time, he himself taunted the rabbi for having followed his advice. For such is the way of the **Yetzer Hara** [evil inclination]: initially he incites a person, and when the person follows him, Heaven forbids, he himself taunts the person afterwards and takes vengeance on him for having listened. May God blessed be He save us from him and bring us back to the truth proper, Amen.

Chapter 9

Wise and Innocent

Once there were two home-owners in a city who had great wealth, large houses and two sons; that is, each one of them had a son. The two children learned together in the same schoolhouse. One of them was a **Chacham** [Torah Scholar] and the other was a **Tam** [Innocent], not that he was a fool; rather, his intellect was simple, without sophistication. The two sons loved each other very much. Even though one was **Chacham** and the other was Tam, they nevertheless loved each other very much.

Came a time when the two householders began to decline. They continued to decline until they lost everything and became destitute with nothing remaining but their houses. As the sons began to grow up, their fathers told them: We do not have enough to pay for you, to sustain you. Do for yourselves what you can. The Tam went and learned shoemaking.

The Chacham, who was a **Bar-Havana** [knowledgeable], an astute, discerning person, didn't want to apply himself to such a common trade. He decided he would travel the world and see what to do. As he was going about the marketplace, he saw a large wagon with four horses in harness speeding through. He called out to the merchants, "Where are you from?"

Sippurei Maasiyot – Chapter 9

They answered him, "From Warsaw." "Where are you going?" "To Warsaw." He asked them, "Perhaps you need workers?" They saw that he was astute, motivated, and looked good. So, they accepted him. He traveled off with them and served them very well on the way.

When they arrived in Warsaw, since he was a Bar-Havana, he decided, "Since I am already in Warsaw, why should I remain with these merchants? Maybe there is a better place than with them. I shall go search and see." As he walked around in the marketplace, he began to investigate and inquire about the men who had brought him, and whether there would be a better place than with them. They answered that these people who had brought him are honest people and it's good to be with them. However, it is very difficult to be with them since their business dealings are in very distant places.

So, he went on. He noticed clothing shop workers as they were going around in the marketplace, with all their customary charm, with their caps and pointy shoes and the rest of the affectations and flair in their gait and appearance. Since he was so sharp and discerning, this occupation looked very proper, being pleasant and local. So, he went to the men who had brought him, gave them his praise and appreciation, but told them that it is not comfortable for him to be with them. As for recompense for them having brought him, he had served them on the road.

Sippurei Maasiyot – Chapter 9

So, he went and offered himself to a proprietor. And the way with servants is, at first one has to be hired for less and do the heavier work. Then later, one advances to better jobs. The proprietor would use him for very hard work, sending him off to nobility carrying merchandise in the manner of servants prominently displaying the garments on their extended arms; this work was very hard for him. Sometimes he needed to carry the merchandise to upper floors, and this work was very hard for him. He decided, since he was a philosopher, a discerning person: "Why do I need this work? Is not the main point the ultimate purpose to get married and make a living? I don't need to see to that yet; I will be free for that later, in the years to come. Meanwhile, it would be better to travel, visiting countries, feasting my eyes on the world."

He went about the marketplace and saw merchants riding on a large wagon. He asked them, "Where are you going?" "To Lagorna." "Would you take me there?" "Yes." They took him there. From there he traveled to Italy, and from there, to Spain.

Meanwhile, many years passed and he became even more knowledgeable on account of having been in many countries. By traveling, a person becomes **Mevin** [discerning]. He decided, "Now, it's time to look at the ultimate purpose." He began to philosophize about what he should do. It seemed to him that he should learn gold smithery, which is a major occupation, a nice craft, entailing great insight and very profitable. And since he was such a Bar-Havana and philosopher, he didn't need to study the trade many years; merely in a quarter year he received the skill, and he became quite a great craftsman, even more of an expert than the one who had trained him. Afterwards he concluded, "Even though I have such a trade in hand, nonetheless I do not have enough with this. Today, this is an important [profession], but maybe at another time some other thing will be considered important." So went ahead and placed himself with a gem cutter. And on account of his cleverness, he acquired this skill in a short time as well - in a quarter year.

Then he philosophically decided, "Even though I have two trades in hand, who knows, perhaps neither of these will remain important. It would be better for me to learn a craft that will always be important." Probing with his insight and philosophy, he determined to learn medicine, which is always needed and always esteemed. Now, the way of learning medicine is to first learn Latin, the language and its writing, as well as the wisdoms of sophistry. And this too, on account of his brilliant mind, he mastered in a short time a quarter year and he became a big doctor, a philosopher and expert in all fields of wisdom.

After all this, the world began to seem, in his eyes, as nil. For due to his genius, and since he was such a great craftsman and so wise and such a doctor, every person in the world was

Sippurei Maasiyot – Chapter 9

like nil to him. He decided that he would now accomplish the purpose and take a wife. He opined to himself: "If I marry here, who will know what has become of me? Let me rather go back home, so that people will see what has become of me. I left as a young boy and now I have come to such greatness." And he picked up and traveled home, experiencing great afflictions on the way. For on account of his sophistication he didn't have anything in common with people about which to converse. He was so worldly and refined that he found no lodging up to his standards and so, he felt constantly afflicted.

For now, let us set aside the story of the clever man. and we will begin to tell the story of the simple man. The simple man learned shoemaking, and since he was a simple person, he had to study the trade a great deal until he got it, and even then, he did not have complete expertise in the craft. He took a wife, and he sustained himself from his work. And since he was a simple person and was not such an expert, therefore his livelihood came with a great deal of pressing and was very limited. He didn't even have time to eat because he always had to work, due to his inability to be more proficient in his craft. Only while he was working when he had inserted the nail and pulled through the cobbler's thread only then would he take a bite of a piece of bread and eat. The simple man's customary behavior was to be always very joyful. He was constantly full

Sippurei Maasiyot – Chapter 9

only of happiness. And he had all the foods, all the drinks and all the clothing. He would say to his wife, "My wife, give me to eat;" and she would give him a piece of bread and he ate. Then he would say, "Give me the sauce with buckwheat groats," and she would cut him off another slice of bread and he ate. And he would praise and say, "How very good and nice is this sauce!" Similarly, he would order himself served meat and other delicacies, and for each dish, she would give him a slice of bread from which he would have great pleasure and give great praise. "How well prepared this is!" as if he had actually eaten that very dish. For he would really and truly feel, in the bread that he ate, the taste of all the foods he wanted; on account of his great **Temimuth** [Innocence] and his immense joy.

And similarly, he would say - My wife, give me a drink of beer; she would give him water and he would praise. How nice is this beer! Then he would summon. Give me mead; she gave him water and he would praise it the same way. Give me wine or other drink; she gave him water and he would delight in and praise the drink as if he really drank the wine, etc.

So too with clothing. He and his wife shared one **Peltz** [fur coat]. He would say, "My wife, give me the **Peltz**, when he needed it namely, to go to the market. She would give him the Peltz. When he needed a **Tulep** [fancy fine fur collar] to go out socially, he would say, "My wife, give me the **Tulep**," and she would give him the **Peltz**. He would take great delight in it and praise, "What a beautiful **Tulep** this is!" When he needed a **Kaftan** [long coat] for instance, to go to synagogue, he would summon and say, "My wife, give me the **Kaftan**," and she would give him the **Peltz**. He would praise and say, "How nice and beautiful is this **Kaftan**!" And so too when he needed to don a **Yupa** [a long silk robe] she would also give him the **Peltz**, and he would also give praise and delight: "How beautiful and nice is this Yupa!" And the like. Thus, he was full only of joy and delight constantly.

When he would finish a shoe, and the shoe probably had three corners. since he did not have complete proficiency in his craft - he would take the shoe in his hand and praise it highly. And he would take great pleasure from it and would say, "My wife, how beautiful and wonderful is this shoe! How sweet it is! What a honey, what a sugary shoe this is!" She would ask him, "If that is so, why do other shoemakers take three gulden for a pair of shoes, and you take only a half thaler one and a half gulden?" He replied, "What's that to me? That's the other person's business and this is my business. And besides, why do we have to talk about other people? Let's just start calculating how much I earn with this shoe "from hand to hand" from his hand to the hand of the customer, considering all factors in the process of making and selling the shoe. The leather costs me this much, tar and thread cost this much, the filling

Sippurei Maasiyot – Chapter 9

between the skins this much, and likewise other items this much; comes out that I profit ten groschen from hand to hand. And with such a profit from hand to hand, what is there to be concerned about?"

So, he was only happy and cheerful at all times, but to the world he was a laughingstock; in him, they had just what they wanted someone to mock however they pleased, for he seemed like a lunatic. People would come and start speaking with him intending to make fun and mock. And the simple man would say to them, "Just without mockery." And as soon as they answered him, "No kidding," he listened to them and started talking with them, for he did not want to further suspect witticisms - that perhaps this itself [their reply] is mockery - for he was a tam. But when he would see that their intention was indeed to ridicule, he would say, "So what if you are cleverer than me? Would you not then be the real fool? For what do I amount to? So, if you'll be cleverer than me, you'll still be a fool!" All this were the usual ways of the simple man. Now we will return to the original subject the **clever man**.

In the meantime, there was a commotion the clever man is traveling and coming here with great pomp and sophistication! The simple man also came running to greet him with great joy. He said to his wife, "Give me quick the **Yupa**! I shall go and greet my dear friend; I will see him." She gave him the **Peltz** and he ran to greet him. Now the clever man was riding

Sippurei Maasiyot – Chapter 9

pompously in a horse-drawn carriage; the simple man came out to greet him and welcomed him joyously, with great love, "My dear brother, how do you do? Blessed is God for bringing you and giving me the privilege of seeing you!" And the clever man, for whom the entire world was like nothing, as was stated above that everyone and everything in the world was insignificant to him, for he considered himself above all the world - all the more so such a person as the tam who seems crazy. But nonetheless, on account of their shared childhood love, he drew him close and traveled with him into town.

Now the two householders, the fathers of these two sons, had died during the time when the clever son was traveling the world. Their houses had been left as an inheritance. The simple son, who had remained local, moved into his father's house claiming his inheritance. The clever son, however, had been in foreign countries and had no one to receive the house. So, the clever man's house became ruined and was lost nothing remained of it. Thus, the clever man had no house to enter when he arrived. He traveled to an inn but was anguished there because it wasn't up to his standards. The simple man now found himself a new occupation he would constantly run from his house to the clever man with love and joy. He noticed that the clever man was suffering from the lodgings. So, the simple man said to the clever man, "Brother, come over to my

Sippurei Maasiyot – Chapter 9

house and stay with me! I will gather all my belongings into one bundle and you'll have my entire house at your disposal." This was agreeable to the clever man, so he moved into his house and stayed with him.

Now the clever man was always full of suffering, for he had left behind a reputation of being a wondrous sage, an artist, and a great doctor. A nobleman came and ordered him to make him a gold ring. He made him quite a wonderful ring and etched out engravings in very amazing ways. He engraved in it a tree that was a total marvel. The nobleman came and the ring did not please him at all. He had enormous suffering because he knew, in himself, that if this ring with the tree would be in Spain, it would be esteemed as an amazing work of art. And similarly, one time a great nobleman came and brought a rare precious gem, brought from distant lands. He also brought with him another gemstone with an engraved image and bid him to etch out that exact image onto the rare gemstone he had brought from distant lands. The **Chacham** [clever man] precisely engraved that exact image, except he made a mistake in one thing which nobody at all would discern except him alone. The nobleman came and took the gem and he liked it very much. But the clever man had great agony from his mistake, "As smart as I am, and this mistake should happen?!"

And similarly in his doctoring, he suffered as well: when he came to an ill person and he gave

Sippurei Maasiyot – Chapter 9

him treatments of which he knew clearly that if the patient would only survive, it would certainly have to be these treatments through which he had healed, for it was an excellent course of treatment. Then, however the patient died. The public said that he died because of him, and he had huge suffering from this. Likewise, sometimes he gave an ill person treatment and the ill person became healthy, and the public said that it was a chance occurrence. So, he was always filled with pain. Similarly, when he needed a garment. He summoned the tailor and took pains with him until he taught him to make the garment to his specifications, according to his knowledge of fashion. The tailor understood the directions and made the garment just as he wanted, except on one lapel, he erred by not shaping it well. The **Chacham** [clever man] suffered great anguish from that because he knew in himself that, although here it would be considered handsome, because no one would perceive [the defect], but "if I were to be in Spain with this lapel, I would be a laughingstock and I would look like an imbecile." And so, he was always full of suffering.

The simple man would joyously run over to the clever man all the time; but he always found him afflicted and full of suffering. He asked him, "How could it be? A wise and wealthy person such as you - why do you always have anguish? Look! Am I not constantly happy?" This was a big joke in the eyes of the clever

Sippurei Maasiyot – Chapter 9

man. The tam seemed crazy to him. The simple man said to him, "Even plain people, when they make fun of me, are fools as well, for if they're already smarter than me, they are first fools themselves as mentioned above! All the more so such a clever person as you. So, what if you are smarter than me?" The simple man spoke up, saying to the clever man, "May the One Who gives grant that you should come up to my level and become a simple person!" The clever man replied, "It is possible that I could reach your level - if my intellect would be taken away, God spare us; or if I became sick, God forbid, I could also become insane. For what are you anyway, but a madman? But that you would come up to my level? No way! It is completely impossible that you would become wise like me!" The simple man answered, "With Hashem Blessed Be He, everything is possible. It could happen in the blink of an eye that I ascend to your [level of brilliance]." The clever man-made great fun of him.

Now these two sons were known in public by their nicknames: **"Khakham**-Clever" and **"Tam**-Simple." Even though there are many clever and simple people in the world, still, in this case, it was unusually apparent. For they were both from the same town, went to school together, and the one had become such an extraordinary genius, while the other was so extremely simple. Even in the public registry the book listing the citizens where they record everyone's given name and family name, these

Sippurei Maasiyot – Chapter 9

two were registered only by their nicknames- **Khakham** and **Tam**. One time, the king was perusing the registry and found these two recorded solely by their nicknames, Clever and Simple. The king was amazed and very much wanted to see them. He realized, "If I suddenly send for them to come before me, they will be very frightened. The clever one won't know at all what to make of this, and the simple man might go crazy from fear." So, the king decided to send a **khakham** to the **khakham** and a tam to the tam. But where does one get a tam in the royal capital city? For in the royal city where the king lives the majority are smart people. However, the one who is appointed overseer of the treasury - he is intentionally a simple person. For they do not want to appoint a clever person overseer of the treasury. Perhaps through his cleverness and his intellect he will embezzle all the funds; therefore, they expressly put a simple person in charge of the treasury.

The king summoned a clever man and the above-mentioned simple man the treasurer, and sent them to the two sons. He gave each one a letter. And he gave them an additional letter to the provincial governor under whose authority the two sons dwelt. In it, the king commanded that the governor should send letters of his own to the clever son and the simple son so that they shouldn't be frightened. He should write to them that the matter is not obligatory, that the king is not explicitly decreeing that they should come, but rather the choice is theirs: if they want, they should come. Just that the king desires to see them.

The emissaries traveled off, the clever one and the simple one, arriving at the governor, delivering the letter. The governor inquired after the two sons. They told him that the **khakham** is an extraordinarily clever person, quite a wealthy man and the "tam" is an exceedingly simple person who believes he has every kind of garment from the single **peltz** [piece of fur] as mentioned before. The governor took counsel that it is certainly inappropriate to bring him before the king dressed in a peltz. So, he arranged for appropriate garments and placed them in the simple man's carriage. And he gave them the aforementioned letters. The messengers traveled off and arrived there. They delivered the letters to them; the clever one delivered to the **khakham** and the simple one to the "tam." Now the **tam**, as soon as he was delivered the letter, spoke up to emissary who was also simple, as above saying, "See here. I don't know what is written in the letter. Read it to me." He answered him, "I'll tell you by memory, what is written in it. The king wants you to come to him." Immediately he asked, "Are you making fun of me?" He answered him, "It is the absolute truth; no kidding. The **tam** was instantly filled with joy and ran, saying to his wife, "My wife, the king has sent for me!" She asked him, "What is it about?

Sippurei Maasiyot – Chapter 9

Why has he sent for you?!" He had no time to answer her at all. He immediately and joyfully rushed off to travel with the emissary, right away entering and sitting down in the carriage. There he found the above-mentioned clothes and he became happier and happier.

In the meantime, reports were sent that the governor was corrupt, and the king deposed him. The king made up his mind: it would be good to have a simple person be governor, for a tam would conduct the country with truth and justice, since he would not know any sophisticated or contriving ways. So, the king decided that he should make the above-mentioned simple son the governor. He issued orders that the **tam**, for whom he had already sent, be appointed governor immediately upon entering the provincial capital. For that would be the route the **tam** must travel. Therefore, they should watch the city gates so that as soon as the **tam** arrives, they should detain him and install him as governor. They did so. They stood over the gates and as soon as he drove through, they stopped him and told him that he had been appointed governor. He inquired, saying, "Please don't clown around with me." They answered him, "Of course! No joking at all! The "tam" immediately became governor, with authority and power.

Now that his mazal went up [mazal - constellation; lit. **flow**; one's destiny or potential as provided by God via arrangement of the constellations] - and as the Talmud teaches, mazal waiting as the mazal flow goes up, so does one's wisdom the **tam** acquired a bit of discernment. Nonetheless, he did not make use of his wisdom at all but just conducted himself with his **Temimuth** [simplicity] as before, and he led the state with Temimuth, with truth and with integrity, with not a drop of corruption. For management of state requires no great intellect nor special knowledge, just uprightness and Temimuth. When two people came before the **tam** for judgment, he would say, "You are innocent and you are liable," purely according to his simplicity and truthfulness, without any crookedness nor deceit. And thus, he conducted everything truthfully.

The country loved him very much and he had loyal advisers who truly loved him. And on account of love, one of them advised him: "Inasmuch as you will certainly be summoned to appear before the king and behold, he has already sent for you and moreover, the procedure is that a governor has to come before the king. Now, even though you are very sincere and the king will not find any fault in you of your leadership of the country, still however it is the routine of the king, when he converses that he digresses into discussing philosophy and languages. Therefore, it will be pleasing and of proper etiquette if you are able to respond to him; therefore, it will be good for me teach you philosophy and languages." The simple man accepted this saying, "Why shouldn't I learn the wisdom of philosophy and languages?" It immediately came to his mind that his friend, the clever man had said to him that it would be impossible in any manner that he should reach his level. "Here I have already arrived at his wisdom!" And still even though he now knew wisdom, he did not use the wisdom at all, but rather conducted himself only with simplicity as before.

Afterwards the king dispatched that the **tam**, the governor, should come to him. He traveled to him. At first, the king discussed the leadership of the country with the **tam**, and the king was very well pleased. For the king saw that he was conducting himself justly and with great honesty, without any wrongdoing or scheming. Then the king began speaking about wisdom and languages; the simple man replied appropriately, and the king was even more pleased. The king said, "I see that he is such a smart person and yet conducts himself with such innocence." The king esteemed him more and more, ending up making him the minister over all the ministers; mandating a special place for him to stay, and commanded to wall him about with very beautiful walls as is befitting, and gave him a writ of appointment that he be chief minister. And so it was; they built him very fine beautiful buildings in the place where the king had ordered, and he received his sovereignty with full effect.

The khakham the clever man. When the letter from the king came to the **khakham**, he replied to the clever person who had delivered it, "Wait. Spend the night here. We'll talk it over and we'll come to a decision." That evening, he prepared him a great feast. During the meal the **khakham** waxed wise, analyzing with his cleverness and philosophy. He spoke up and said, "What can this mean, that such a king should send for such a lowly person as me? What am I that the king should send for me? Such a king with such authority and prestige! And me, so insignificant and despicable compared with such a great king - well, how is it conceivable that such a king should send for so unimportant a person as me? If I should say on account of my wisdom, what am I next to the king? What! The king doesn't have any wise men? Moreover, the king is certainly a great sage himself. So, what is this, that the king should send for me?" He was very, very astonished by this. He spoke up, saying that is, the original **khakham**, who was the simple man's childhood friend for all this conjecture was the original **khakham's** monologue describing his astonishment and surprise, to which he now answers his own rhetoric, saying to the clever messenger, "You know what I say? My opinion is that it clearly must be that there is no king whatsoever in the world. That the entire world is mistaken in this foolishness; that they think there is a king. See! Understand - how can it be possible that the entire world should give itself over to depend on one man, that he should be the king? There is certainly

Sippurei Maasiyot – Chapter 9

no king in the world at all".

The clever messenger replied, "Haven't I brought you a letter from the king?" The original **khakham** asked him, "Did you yourself receive the letter from the king's hand directly?" He answered him, "No. Just another person gave me the letter in the king's name." He answered up, saying, "Now see with your own eyes that my words are correct that there is absolutely no king." He returned to asking him, "tell me, are you not from the capital city and did you not grow up there all your life? Tell me, have you ever, in all your days, seen the king?" He answered, "No." For in fact, it is so, that not everyone is privileged to see the king, for the king does not reveal himself publicly except on rare occasion. The original **khakham** declared, "Now open your eyes and see that I am correct, that there is definitely no king whatsoever, for even you have never seen the king." Once again, the messenger answered the **khakham**, "If it is really so, who then rules the country?" The first **khakham** responded, "That - I'll make clear to you, for it is specifically me you should ask, since I am an expert in this. I have wandered about in many countries; I've been to Italy. The customary practice is that there are seventy ministerial advisers' senators who go up and lead the country for a certain time. Then the authority is given over to the next group until each and every resident takes a turn." His words started to penetrate into the clever messenger's ears

Sippurei Maasiyot – Chapter 9

until they came to agree and conclude that there definitely is no king in the world at all.

The original **khakham** furthermore declared, "Come! Let us travel the world; I will show you more how the entire world is in great error." They went and traveled the world and wherever they arrived they always found the public in error. The matter of the king became an example for them. In other words, just like the public was in error in their belief in the existence of the king, so too everything held to be true by the populace must be mistaken. With this attitude, they traveled the world until they ran out of money and supplies. They began by selling one horse and then the other until they had sold everything and had to go on foot. Incessantly they kept examining the world, finding fault. They became poor vagrants, their status disintegrated, for no one would give consideration to such paupers.

The circumstances played out that they were wandering about until they came to the city in which the minister lived that is, the **tam**, the simple man, the friend of the **khakham**, the clever man. There in that city was a genuine Baal Shem [lit. Master of the Divine Name; a holy man and miracle worker]. The Baal Shem was held in high esteem because he had done truly amazing things, and even among the nobility he was important and famous. The two clever men came into the city, walked about and came before the house of the Baal Shem. They saw many wagons stationed there forty or

Sippurei Maasiyot – Chapter 9

fifty with sick people. The **khakham** figured that a doctor must live there. He wanted to go into the house, for since he too was a great doctor, he wanted to go in to make his acquaintance. He asked, "Who lives here?" They answered him, "A Baal Shem." This filled his mouth with laughter and he said to his friend, "This is another lie and an outrageous mistake! This is even more nonsense than the mistake about the king! Brother, let me tell you about this fallacy, how very much the world is fooled by this lie.

Meanwhile they became hungry and found that they still had three or four groschen. They went into a soup-kitchen type **Everyman's-Kitchen** [Restaurant] where food is available for even three, four groschen. They ordered food and they were served. While they were eating, they talked and made fun of the **lie** and the **error** of the matter of the Baal Shem. The **Gorkekher** [Restaurant-Owner] heard their talk and was very annoyed, because the Baal Shem was highly esteemed there. He said to them, "Eat up what you have and get out of here." Then a son of the Baal Shem arrived there, and they kept on ridiculing the Baal Shem right in front of his son. The restaurateur growled at them for making fun of the Baal Shem in front of his son, until he lashed out, beating them with injurious blows, and shoved them out of his home. It made them furious and they wanted to seek judgment against the one who had beaten them. They decided to go to

Sippurei Maasiyot – Chapter 9

their innkeeper, where they had left their luggage, to take counsel with him as to how to obtain judgement for the above assault. They came and told him that the restaurateur had severely beaten them. He asked them, "Why did he hit you?" They told him that they had spoken against the Baal Shem. He responded, "It definitely is not right to hit people, but you behaved completely improperly by talking against the Baal Shem, for the Baal Shem is highly regarded here." They saw that he was not for real, that he too was in "error." They left him and went to the city clerk, who was a gentile. They told him the story that they had been beaten. He asked, "What for?" They responded that they had spoken against the Baal Shem. The clerk beat them bloody and shoved them out of his office.

They went from this one to that one, each time to a higher authority until they came before the above-mentioned minister. There, in front of the ministry, were stationed soldiers, i.e., sentries. They announced to the minister that a person needs him, and he ordered him to enter. The **khakham** came before the minister who immediately recognized him, that this **khakham** is none other than his friend. However, the **khakham** did not recognize the **tam** due to his superior status.

Immediately the minister initiated, saying to him, "See my **Temimuth** [my simplicity], to what it has brought me - to greatness such as this! And to what has your cleverness brought you?" The **khakham** spoke up and said, "That it turns out that you are my friend, the tam - about this we can speak later. Right now, give me a judgement against them for having hit me." He asked him, "Why did they hit you?" He answered him, "Because I spoke against the Baal Shem, that he is a lie and a great fraud." Answered up the tam prime minister saying, "You still adhere to your contrivances? Look, you once said you could easily reach my level, but I could not reach yours. Now see that I have already long reached your level, as mentioned above [that the tam had already become exceedingly wise as well] but you still have not reached mine. And I see that it is far more difficult for you to come to my **Temimuth** [level of simplicity]." However, since the tam minister had known him from long ago when the **khakham** was still great, he ordered that he be given garments in which to be attired and he bid that he dine with him.

While they were eating, they began to converse, the **khakham** started trying to prove his aforementioned opinion that there is no king at all. The tam minister snarled at him, "What!? I myself have seen the king!" The **khakham** answered him glibly, "Do you know personally that it was the king? Do you know him, his father and his grandfather to have been kings? From where do you know that this is the king? People have told you that this is the king. They have deceived you with a lie." The tam became deeply vexed about the king, that he

Sippurei Maasiyot – Chapter 9

should deny the king's existence.

Meanwhile someone came and said, "The **Devil** [Azazel] has sent for you plural." The tam shook with terror and ran and told his wife with great trepidation how the Devil had sent for him. She advised him to send for the Baal Shem. He sent for him; the Baal Shem came and gave him **kame`as** [amulets containing holy names] and other protections and told him that he need no longer fear at all. He had great faith in this. So, the **khakham** and the tam were again sitting together as before. The **khakham** asked him, "What were you so terrified about?" He answered him, "Because of the Devil, who had sent for us." The **khakham** ridiculed him, "You believe that there is a Devil?!" He responded, "If not, then who sent for us?" The **khakham** answered him, "This is definitely my brother. He wanted to be seen with me, and set up a scam to send for me." The tam asked him, "If this is so, how did he get past all the sentries?" He answered him, "He certainly bribed them, and they are saying fraudulently the lie that they did not see him at all." Meanwhile again someone came and said as before, "The Devil has sent for you." This time, the simple man was not shaken at all and had no fear whatsoever, on account of the protections from the Baal Shem. He spoke up, saying to the **khakham**, "Now what do you say?" He said, "I will inform you that I have a brother who is angry at me. He has set up this scam in order to frighten me." He stood and asked the one who had come for them, "What does he look like, the one who sent for us? Which type of facial [structure] and hairstyle does he have, etc., and the like. He answered him, such and such. The **khakham** answered up, saying, "See! That is my brother's appearance!" The tam said to him, "Will you go with them?" He responded, "Yes. Just give me a few soldiers as **Zalaga** [escorting guards] so that they shouldn't hurt me." He gave him a zalaga and the two clever men the original **khakham** and the messenger went with the man who had come for them. The soldiers of the zalaga returned and the tam, the minister asked them, "Where are those sophisticates?" They replied that they do not know at all how they disappeared. The Devil had snatched those two sophisticates and carried them off to a place of slime and mud. There the Devil would sit on a throne amidst the muck. He threw them into the mire which was thick and sticky, literally like glue, and they were completely unable to move in the muck. They these clever guys screamed at those who were afflicting them, that is the Devil and his henchmen, "Wicked ones! What are you torturing us for? Is there really a Devil in the world? You are evil, torturing us for no reason!" For these smart men still did would not believe that there is a Devil; instead, they insisted that evil thugs were persecuting them without cause. The two sophisticates were left in the thick mire and were trying to figure out, "What is this? These

Sippurei Maasiyot – Chapter 9

are nothing but hooligans with whom we had once quarreled, and now they are afflicting us so harshly." They remained there, tortured and horribly abused for a number of years.

One time the **tam** the simple man who became the prime minister passed by the Baal Shem's home and was reminded of his friend, the **khakham**, the clever man. He went in to the Baal Shem and leaned in to him as is the way of officials wishing not to be overheard, asking whether it would be possible to show him the **khakham** and whether he could extricate him. He said to the Baal Shem, "Do you remember the **khakham** whom the Devil sent for and carried away, and who has not been seen since?" He answered him, "Yes." He bid him to please show him the place of the **khakham** and to extricate him from there. The Baal Shem said to him, "I can certainly show you his place and take him out. Only no one but you and I may go." So, they went together. The Baal Shem did what he knew to transcend space and time in order to locate and go to the place and they arrived there. He saw how they lay there in the thick muck and slime. When the **khakham** noticed the minister, he screamed to him, "Brother, look! They are beating and torturing me so intensely these hooligans for no reason!" The minister snarled at him, "Still, you hold to your contrivances and don't want to believe in anything at all?! You say these are people?? Now see here! Look! This is the Baal Shem whom you had denied. He is specifically

Sippurei Maasiyot – Chapter 9

the one who can take you out and he will show you the truth." The tam, the minister, beseeched the Baal Shem to take them out and show them that this is the Devil and that these are not humans.

The Baal Shem did what he did, and they were left standing on the dry land with no mire there at all. And the damaging demons became plain dust. Then the **khakham** saw and begrudgingly was forced to admit to everything, that there is indeed a king and there is indeed a genuine Baal Shem, etc.

Rav Nosson adds the following: Regarding this story of **Rebbe Nachman** gave over the teaching, which discusses **khakhmoth** [wisdoms, sophistication, cleverness] and temimuth, innocence that the essence of personal wholeness is only **Temimuth V'pshituth** [innocence and simplicity]. It further discusses the matter of Amalek who was the epitome of a **khakham** casting doubt through constant clever over-analysis, who heretically denied the main point [Hashem and the True Purpose of life] etc. See there on the verse in Mishlei - ShevA yipoL tzaddiM wekaM - [Seven times the tzaddik falls, but rises] - the end letters of each word spell out **AMaLeK**. For the main reason for spiritual falls is **Khokhmoth** [cleverness always trying to be smart in analyzing and figuring out everything]. Likewise, King Agag, who was a descendant of Amalek, even though he could see his imminent downfall when Samuel

Sippurei Maasiyot – Chapter 9

arrived... to execute him, he still did not believe, as it says - "Agag went ma'adanoth" which **Targum Yonatan** [Translates] as "went in a self-indulgent manner." For he still did not believe in his immanent demise. Not until the very end did, he see his vanquishment with his eyes, as then he says, "Has the bitterness of death indeed turned unto me?" For until then, he still did not believe.

If you will look into this tale, you will perceive wonder of wonders: And if prayer is not as it needs to be, this is an example of the "three cornered shoe". Understand this well. And see also at the end of the book the Rav's explanation, and you will see wonderful analogous commentaries.

Chapter 10

The Burgher and the Pauper

Once there was a **Burgher** [Great merchant] class in Medieval Europe. burgh denotes a fortified city and is related to the word berg, mountain; see Rabbi Nathan's notes at the story's end who was an extremely rich man and had a vast amount of merchandise. **Vekhseln** [His promissory notes] and letters of **Briv** [credit] circulated over the world and he had everything good. Below him lived a pauper who was an extremely poor man and had the complete opposite of the burgher that is, the complete reverse: just as the burgher was a very rich man, so the pauper was conversely a very poor man. But both of them had no children: the burgher had no children and likewise the pauper also had no children. Once, the burgher dreamed that people came to his house and were making packages and packages. He asked them, "What are you doing?" They replied: they will carry it all away to that very same pauper, that is, the pauper who lived under him, as mentioned. It annoyed him very much and he grew very angry that they wanted to carry away all his wealth to the pauper. To be wroth at them was impossible, for they were a good many people. So, they continued making packages and packages of all his belongings, all his wares

Sippurei Maasiyot – Chapter 10

and all his goods and they carried absolutely everything away to the aforementioned pauper, leaving him nothing in the house but the bare walls; and it upset him very, very much. Meanwhile, he woke up and saw: it's a dream. And even though he saw it's only a dream and, thank God, all his belongings were with him - still all the same his heart pounded mightily and the dream could not be got out of his mind and the dream upset him severely. The pauper and his wife used to be cared for by the burgher and he would give to them often. But now after the dream he cared for them more than before. However, whenever the poor man or his wife would come into his house, his facial expression would change and he became frightened of them because he would recall the dream. And they, that is, the pauper and his wife, would often go to his house and were often with him.

One time the pauper's wife came to his house and he gave her what he gave her, and his expression changed and he became stricken with fear. She asked him and said, "I beg pardon of your honor. Tell me why it is that whenever we come to you your face becomes drastically changed." He told her the whole story: that he had had such a dream as above and since then his heart has been pounding him mightily as above. She replied to him: did the dream take place on such and such a night which she said? He answers her, "Yes. What about it?" She replies to him, "On that night I

Sippurei Maasiyot – Chapter 10

also dreamed: that I'm a very wealthy person, and people had come to my house and were making packages upon packages. I asked them, where are you bringing this?' They replied, To the pauper that is, to the burgher, whom they already called a poor man now. Therefore, why do you pay attention to a dream? What for? - I also had a dream." Now the burgher has become all the more frightened and confused, since he has heard her dream as well, because it seems that his wealth and property are to be brought to the pauper and that the pauper's poverty are to be brought to him. He has become extremely panicked.

And the day came to pass - the burgher's wife took a trip by coach, taking other wives along with her, and she took the pauper's wife too. And while traveling along on their tour, meanwhile a general and his army passed through. They got off the road and the army passed through. The general saw that women were traveling and he gave orders that one of them should be taken out, and they went and took out the pauper's wife, snatched her into the general's coach and drove away with her. Getting her back was certainly impossible now, for he had driven off with her, and especially a general with his army... …. And with her he rode to his country. And she was a Heaven-fearing person that is, she had fear of God and she was not willing to listen to him at all and she wept very profusely. They implored her a great deal and coaxed her but she was,

Sippurei Maasiyot – Chapter 10

however, an exceedingly Heaven-fearing person. And she the burgher's wife, and the other wives, returned from their tour but the pauper's wife was not there. The pauper wept very, very much, beating his head against the wall and constantly mourning for his wife bitterly.

One day the burgher passed by the pauper's house and heard the poor man crying so bitterly and beating his head against the wall. He went in and asked him, "Why are you crying so intensely?" He answered him, "Why shouldn't I weep? What do I have left? Some people are left with wealth or with children. I have nothing at all and my wife has also been taken from me. What do I have left?" The burgher's heart was very touched, and he had great pity on the pauper on account of seeing his bitterness, his acute sorrow, and he went and did a reckless thing; it was so truly an insanity - and he went and asked in which city the general lives, and he journeyed there. Then he did a reckless [Heb. mevohal me'od very panicked] thing: going into the general's house. Now, before the general there are sentries posted, but he the burgher, on account of his severe agitation, suddenly with extreme turmoil went and paid no attention to the guards whatsoever; and the guards became shocked and extremely confused due to suddenly seeing a man beside them in great agitation, so they became very shocked: "How did this guy get here?" And due to their panic, all the guards permitted him and

Sippurei Maasiyot – Chapter 10

he passed through all the guards until he went in the general's house, in the place where she, the pauper's wife, was lying. And he came and woke her up, and said to her, "Come!" When she caught sight of him, she took fright. He said to her, "Come with me right away!" She went with him, and now again they passed by all the guards until they emerged outside. Only then did he first come around and realize what he had done there, such a wild thing, and he realized that for certain there would right away be a big uproar at the general, and that's just what happened: there was a big commotion at the generals. The burgher went and hid himself with her in a pit where there was rainwater until the commotion died down, and he tarried there with her for two days. She saw the great self-sacrifice that he has for her sake and the troubles that he suffers for her, and she swore by God that all the mazall that she has - possibly she has some kind of mazal, that she will have supreme grandeur and **Hatzlocheh** [success] - then all her success will not be withheld from him that is, from the burgher, and that if he should want to take for himself all her success and greatness, so that she should remain just as she was before, it would not be withheld from him whatsoever. However, how does one get witnesses there? She took the pit as a witness.

After two days he went out of there with her and went further. And he went with her further and further. And he understood that there in that place, he is also being sought. He went and hid himself with her in a mikveh ritual bath. There once again she recalled the great sacrifice and the suffering which he endures for her sake and she once again swore as before: that all her mazal etc. as mentioned, taking the ritual bath as her witness. They were there as well for approximately two days and they went out and went further. Again, he understood that they are searching here too and again he hid himself along with her. And so, it happened several times, hiding himself with her each time in another place, namely in seven different waters, that is, in a pit with water and in a mikveh as mentioned, and ponds mucky waters, a spring, **Rivulets** [creeks], rivers and seas. And in every place where they hid, she kept remembering his self-sacrifice and the troubles which he endures for her sake, and she kept swearing: that her mazal etc. as mentioned, each time taking the place as witness, as mentioned. And they kept going in this manner, always hiding themselves in those places mentioned above, until they came to the sea. When they came to the sea - and the burgher was a great merchant and knew the sea lanes - he negotiated to get to his country, until he traveled the way and came home with the pauper's wife and brought her back to the pauper. There was great rejoicing. The burgher, because he had done such a thing, and in addition had withstood trial passed the test with her that is, he had the fear of God and did not

Sippurei Maasiyot – Chapter 10

touch her, therefore he was "remembered". And that year he had a son. And she too, that is, the pauper's wife, because she withstood such a trial, both with the general and with the burgher, she therefore merited to have a daughter. And she was a supreme beauty, an extraordinarily great beauty which was unlike any human beauty whatsoever, for among mankind one never sees such beauty. Everyone would say, "She should just grow to maturity!" for it is hard for such an extraordinary novelty to reach maturity, because her beauty was absolutely extraordinary, the likes of which one doesn't see on earth. Everyone in the world would travel in and come to see her, and they would be very astonished at her beauty which was very, very extraordinary, and would give her gifts all the time out of affection, and they so kept presenting gifts until the pauper became rich .

As for the burgher, it entered his mind that he should arrange a match with the pauper due to her great beauty which was such a marvel, and he thought to himself: maybe this is what the dream will mean; that what's his is brought to the pauper and what's the pauper's to him; maybe the dream signifies this, that they will have a match; they will be mixed into one through the match.

One time, the pauper's wife came to the burgher and he told her that he has desire to have a match with her; and maybe through this the dreams will be realized, as above. She

Sippurei Maasiyot – Chapter 10

replied to him, "I've had this in mind as well, but I didn't have the boldness to talk of this, that I should be related to you through marriage. But if you want, I am certainly ready and will certainly not hold back from you, for I have already sworn that all my good and my success will not be withheld from you. And the son of the burgher and the daughter both learned in one schoolroom, languages and other things as was the order among them. And people would come to see the daughter on account of the exceptional novelty and kept presenting her with gifts until the pauper became rich.

And nobility would come see her and they liked her very much, and her beauty was an extreme marvel, for it was no human kind of beauty; and because of her extraordinary beauty the nobility got the idea of contracting a marriage with the pauper, and any minister who had a son wanted very much to contract a marriage with her. However, it would not befit the nobility to have a match with him that is, with the pauper; they therefore needed to see to exerting themselves to make this man big that is, the pauper, and they saw to it that he should perform a service for the **Caesar** [Emperor]. And he was first an ensign [flag] and afterwards continually higher and higher, for they saw to it to quickly promote him each time, until he rapidly became each time higher and higher, until he became a general. By now the nobility already wanted to have a match with him, however there were many nobilities

Sippurei Maasiyot – Chapter 10

who wanted this, for many nobilities had aimed at this, and busied themselves with it, to continuously promote him. Therefore, he could not have a match with any of them. And furthermore, he could not have a match with any of them on account of the burgher, for it was already discussed that there would be a match with him.

And the pauper, who has now become a general - he became more and more successful. And the emperor would send him into battles and he was successful each time, and the emperor promoted him still higher each time and he was continuously very successful, until the emperor died. The entire country came to the decision to make him emperor, and all the nobility assembled together and all agreed that he should be emperor. He became emperor that is, the aforementioned pauper has now become emperor and he waged wars and was very successful, conquering countries, and waged more wars and was continuously successful, continually taking over countries until the other lands themselves submitted themselves under him with good will, for they saw his success is extremely great, for all the beauty of the world and all the mazal of the world was with him. So, all the kings met together and agreed that he should be emperor over the entire world, and they gave him a document written with golden letters. And the emperor that is, the pauper who has become emperor over the entire world no longer wanted to have a match with the

Sippurei Maasiyot – Chapter 10

burgher, for it is not fitting that an emperor should have a match with a burgher. But his wife the empress - she did not desert the burgher. That is, she stood by the burgher because he had risked his life for her sake, as mentioned. The emperor therefore saw that he cannot make any match on account of the burgher, particularly since his wife supports him very, very much. Therefore, he began to think thoughts about the burgher; and in the beginning he saw to it to place him in poverty and he made schemes just as if it were not from him at all, and he continually saw to it to cause him damages; and an emperor can certainly do this. He was continually caused losses and continuously beaten out of money until he became impoverished and became an absolute pauper. But she, the empress, kept adhering to the burgher.

Then the emperor realized that as long as the son is alive, that is, the burgher's son he can make no other match. The emperor exerted himself to rid the **Bachur** [young man] from the earth and he thought out plans to eliminate him. And he set up false charges on him and called the judges into session to try him. The judges understood that the emperor's will was that he be eliminated from the world, and they delivered the sentence that he be put in a sack that is, the burgher's son and thrown into the sea. As for the empress, her heart was very pained at this, however, even the empress too can do nothing up against the emperor. She went to the designees who were appointed to throw him into the sea, and she came to them and fell at their feet and pleaded with them direly that they should do for her sake and let him go, for: why does he deserve execution? So, she begged them very much that they should take another captive who had to be executed and throw him into the sea, and the young man they should release. This she achieved with them; they swore that they would release him and so they did. And they took another man and threw him into the sea, but him they released saying: "Go! Go!" And he went away. And the young man was already of mature mind - **Bar da'at** [son of knowledge], so he went his way.

And before this, that is, prior to the young man leaving, the empress went and summoned her daughter and said to her thus: "My daughter, you must know that this burgher's son is your groom;" and she told her daughter the entire story that happened to her, and "how the burgher sacrificed his well-being for my sake and was with me in the seven places that is, in the seven types of water, and I swore to him every time by God that all my good would not be withheld from him, and I took those seven places as witnesses that is, the pit, the mikveh, and all the rest of the seven types of water." Therefore now - you are all my good and all my mazal and my success; you are certainly his, and his son is your groom. And your father because of his haughtiness wants to kill him for

Sippurei Maasiyot – Chapter 10

no reason, but I have already made efforts to save him and have brought about that he be released. Therefore, you should know that he is your groom that is, the burgher's son, and you must not agree to any other groom in the world." The daughter accepted her mother's words, because she too was a God-fearing person, and she replied to her mother that she would certainly uphold her words.

The daughter went and sent a note to the burgher's son in prison, that she retains herself by him and he is her groom. And she sent something like a piece of a map, and she drew on it all the places where her mother had hidden with his father, which are the seven witnesses, that is, the pit, the mikveh and the rest as mentioned; that is, on it she drew something like a pit, a mikveh, and the rest of the seven types of waters. And she ordered him very, very strongly that he should guard this note very, very much, and she signed herself underneath; then things took place as mentioned: the deputies took another man, and him they released and he went on his way. And he went and went until he reached the sea and he boarded a ship and set out upon the sea. A big storm wind came along and carried away the ship to a coast that was desert that is, desolate and on account of the great tempest, the ship was broken up; however, the passengers were saved and made out to dry land. And there it was a wilderness; the people from the ship went off in search of food. Each

Sippurei Maasiyot – Chapter 10

one looked for something to eat, for at that location it was not the norm that ships should arrive there, for it was desert. Therefore, they did not think there, that some ship would come so that they could return home. They went along in the wilderness in search of food and became scattered here and there, each one separate. And the young man wanted to turn back but he no longer could, and the more he wanted to turn back, the farther he got, until he saw he can no longer return; so, he went where he went in the wilderness. And he had in his hand a bow with which he protected himself against the vicious animals of the wilderness, and while walking he found himself something to eat there. And thus, he walked and walked, until he emerged from the wilderness. And he arrived at a habitable spot that was a vacant place, and there was water there, and fruit trees around with fruit, and he ate of the fruit and drank of the water. And he resolved in his mind that he would settle down there for as long as he lives, for after all, anyhow it is already difficult for him to return to civilization, and who knows if he would again arrive at such a place if he would leave this place and go away? Therefore, he wanted to dwell away there, and there live out this world. For it was good for him there, as he had fruit to eat and water to drink; and sometimes he would go out and shoot with his bow a rabbit or a deer and he had meat to eat. And he would catch fish there, for there were very good fish in the water there. It

Sippurei Maasiyot – Chapter 10

pleased him to live out his years there.

As for the emperor, after the sentence had been carried out on the burgher's son and he was now free of him for the emperor thought that they had indeed truly executed the judgment on the young man and he is no longer on the earth, now then he can already make a match with his daughter that is, for his own daughter. They began proposing matches to her with this king and with that king, and he made her a court in the appropriate way, and she remained there. And she took young ladies, daughters of nobility, to be her companions and she lived there, and she would play on musical instruments in their usual fashion. And whatever they proposed match to her, she always replied that she did not want any talk that is, talk about the match but that he himself should come, he who wants to marry her. And she had very expert knowledge of the **Chokhmah** [wisdom] of song that is, the chokhmah to speak very beautiful lyrics with great chokhmah; and with skillful artisanship she made a place for him to come to that is, he who wants to marry her and stand facing her and say a song, that is, a song of desire, just as a desirer speaks to his desired that is, words of love. Kings would come to be matched with her and they arrived at that place and they each one spoke his song.

To some of them she sent a reply through her ladies, also with a song and with affection. And to some whom she liked more, she herself responded and she would raise her voice with a song and reply to him as well words of affection. And to some whom she liked even more she would personally show herself face to face; so, she showed her face and replied to him with a song with affection. But to all of them she always concluded in the end, "The waters, however, did not pass over you." And none of them understood what she meant. And when she showed her face people would fall down due to enormous beauty, and some were left weak and some became insane on account of lovesickness due to her great beauty which was very, very extraordinary. And nonetheless, even though they became insane and were left weak, despite this king would still come to be matched with her; and she gave them all the same answer, as above.

And the burgher's son remained in that same place and he made himself a place to dwell in and he lived there. And he too could play and knew the wisdom of song; he selected wood out of which musical instruments can be made and he made himself instruments, and from the veins of animals he made strings; thus, he would musically accompany himself. And he would take the note that he had which she had sent him at the time he was in captivity and he would sing and play and remember what had befallen him, and how his father had been a burgher etc., and now he has been cast off to here. And he went and took the note and made a sign on a tree and made a place there in the

Sippurei Maasiyot – Chapter 10

tree and hid the note there, and he dwelled there for some time.

One time there was a great storm wind and it broke all the trees that were standing there. He could not recognize the tree where he had hidden the note, for when the trees were standing in their place, he had a sign to recognize, but now that they had fallen the tree became mixed among the other trees which were very numerous there; he could no longer recognize the particular tree. And it was impossible to split open all the trees and look for the note, for there were very many trees. He cried exceedingly and was extremely sad and he realized that if he would stay there, he would certainly become insane on account of great anguish that he had. He came to the decision that he must go further away and whatever should happen to him, let happen - go away he must, for he is anyway in great danger due to severe anguish. So, he got some meat and fruit into a sack and went wherever he would go. And he made signs in the place from which he left and he went along until he reached a settled area. He asked them, "What land is this?" They answered him. He asked if they had heard about the emperor here. They answered him, "Yes." He asked if they had heard about his daughter, the beauty. They answered him, "Yes, but no one can be matched with her as mentioned, for she wants none of them, as mentioned." He came to a decision, since he can't get there anyway - and he went to the king

Sippurei Maasiyot – Chapter 10

of the country and spoke his heart out entirely: And that he is her groom and because of him she wants no other match. And he cannot get there, therefore he gives over to the king all the signs that he has, that is, the seven waters mentioned above. And the king should himself go there and he will match himself with her; and he should give him money for this.

The king recognized that his words are true, for one cannot think up such things out of one's heart. The thing pleased the king. However, he decided: if he brings her here and the young man will be here, this is not good for him. Should he kill him? He did not want to do such a thing, for why should one after all kill him for the favor? Therefore, the king decided he would exile him two hundred miles away. He was very upset at him exiling him for such a favor as he had done him. There as well he went to another king and told likewise too as before. That is, the young man, the burgher's son, because it upset him that the first king exiled him, went to another king and told him as well the whole story with all the signs, so that the other should make haste to marry the beauty. So, he related to him all the signs and to this other king he added an additional sign. And he ordered him and rushed him to set out immediately; maybe he can overtake the other king, in order to get there first; and even if he does not arrive first, he still has one sign more than the first. And the second one decided as well like the first that it is not good for him if

Sippurei Maasiyot – Chapter 10

the young man should be here; the other king also exiled him two hundred miles further. He was again very upset and he went again to a third one that is, the young man, the burgher's son, again went to a king who was now the third, and also told him as before, the entire story; so, he went another time, to a third king. He also told him the whole story, as with the others. And to the third one he gave even more signs, very good signs.

The first king got up and traveled there and arrived there at the location of the emperor's daughter, that is, the beauty. And the king composed a song and embedded in the song, with wisdom, all the places, that is, the seven aforementioned witnesses that is, the seven types of water, which were the essential signs of her groom that she had, as mentioned. However, in accord with the science of song the seven places came out for him not in order that is, for example he had to say the pit first and then the mikveh etc., but he said in reverse, for so it came out for him according to the wisdom of the song. And the king came up on the place that is, on the place where the one who wanted to be matched with her had to come upon and say a song with wisdom as mentioned, and he said his song. When she heard the places that is, the seven types of waters it was extraordinary news for her. It felt to her that this was certainly her groom, but it was difficult for her why he said them not in order. However, notwithstanding, she thought

Sippurei Maasiyot – Chapter 10

perhaps due to the science of the song, this order came out for him. It was accepted in her heart that this is he himself. She wrote to him that she designates herself as matched with him. There was a grand celebration and a commotion inasmuch as the beauty has at last found her match, and they were already preparing for the wedding.

Meanwhile, the other one arrived that is, the other king, to whom the young man had also divulged all the signs plus one more sign, as mentioned. And the other one also ran there and they told him that she has already made a match, but he paid no mind to this [lit. he didn't look at it] and he said: nonetheless, he still has something to tell her; that he will certainly have an effect. He came that is, the other king and said his song - and this other one has now arranged all the places in order, and moreover, he gave one more sign in addition. She asked him, "From where does the first one know?" If he were to tell the truth it would not be good for him that is, the other thought he cannot tell her the truth, that the young man told the first one, for it's not good for him if she should know that. So, he said he doesn't know from where the first one knew the signs. It was a big wonder to her and she was left standing bewildered, for the first one also told out all the places; and from where should a man know these signs? But notwithstanding, it felt to her that this other second one is her groom, for she saw that he told in sequence, and in addition

Sippurei Maasiyot – Chapter 10

one more sign; and the first one, maybe it came out to him through the science of song that he mentioned the places. Albeit, now she remained standing in other words she could no longer give herself counsel; she stayed put and now was not willing to be matched with anyone.

And the young man, that is, the burgher's son, when the second king exiled him, was again very upset, and he went to a third king and told him the whole entire story as above, and he told him even more signs, very good signs. And in front of this third one he told out his entire heart: Inasmuch as he had a note on which all these places were drawn that is, the seven types of water; therefore, the king should draw on a piece of paper all those places and bring it to her. And the third king also exiled the young man two hundred miles further yet, and the third one also ran there. And he got there; he was told that the other two that is, the two kings are there already. He replied, "Nevertheless," for he has such a thing that he will definitely have an effect. And the world people did not know whatsoever why she wants these kings more than others. And the third one came and said his song with very excellent signs, better than the first ones, and he showed the note where he himself had re-drawn the places with all the places drawn. She became very panicked in other words, scared and disturbed, however, she did not at all know a thing to do, since regarding the first one she also thought

Sippurei Maasiyot – Chapter 10

that this is he; and then regarding the second. Therefore, she said that she would believe no longer until her very own writing itself is brought. Then the young man decided that is, the burgher's son: how will he always be sent further away? So, he made up his mind he himself would set out for there that is, to the emperor's daughter; perhaps he will have an effect. And he went and went until he got there. And he said he has something that will definitely have an effect. And he approached and said his song. And he said even more signs, very good signs, and he reminded her that he had learned with her in one schoolroom, and other signs too. And he told her everything: that he had sent the aforementioned kings and hidden the writing in a tree, and everything that had befallen him.

But she did not regard this at all and the first three kings certainly also had to say some reasons for not having the note. And to recognize him is certainly impossible, for a long time had already passed. So, she already no longer wanted to regard any signs at all until the writing of her own hand is brought, for regarding the first one she also thought that this is he for certain, and likewise regarding the second, etc.; therefore, she no longer wanted any signs, etc. as mentioned. And the young man that is, the burgher's son decided he can make no delay whatsoever here in other words, he cannot tarry here, for it may become known that he is here; the emperor will kill him, as

Sippurei Maasiyot – Chapter 10

mentioned. He made up his mind he would again return back to his spot in the wilderness where he was before, and there he would live out his life. And he went and traveled to get to that wilderness and he arrived there at the wilderness. Meanwhile as the above was all happening, very many years went by. And it remained in the young man's mind that he should sit away there in the wilderness and live out his years there. According to how he had evaluated the entire mortal life on earth, it was clear in his mind that it is good for him to live out his years here in the wilderness; and he lived there and ate from the fruits, etc. as mentioned.

Now, on the sea was a murderer, and the murderer heard that there exists such a beauty on the earth. He wanted to abduct her even though he did not need her since he was a eunuch; he only wanted to grab her in order to sell her to some king; he'll get a great deal of money for her. So, the murderer began to busy himself with the thing. And a murderer is a reckless person, so he abandoned himself: if he accomplishes, he accomplishes, and if not, what will he forfeit here? For he is after all a reckless person, as the way of a murderer is. So, the murderer went and bought a vast number of wares - extraordinarily much. And he made golden birds, and they were made with craftsmanship so that one would think they live; they were just like living birds in nature. Moreover, he made golden grain stalks, and the

Sippurei Maasiyot – Chapter 10

birds stood on the grain stalks and this alone was a novelty, that the birds stand on the stalks without the stalks breaking, for they were large birds. And furthermore, he made devices so that a person thought that the birds make music; one-clicked its tongue, one chirped, and once sang. And this was all done with cunning, for men stood there in a room that was on the ship and the men stood under the birds and the men did it all, and it was thought that the birds themselves make music, for they were cunningly made with wires; it was thought the birds themselves do all this.

And the murderer went off with all this to the land where the aforementioned emperor's daughter was. And he came to the city where she was and he brought himself to a standstill with the ship in the sea and anchored the ship and made himself out to be a big merchant. People would go to him to buy expensive wares, and he stayed there a while, a quarter year and longer, and people always carried off beautiful wares that they bought from him. The emperor's daughter also desired to buy wares from him; she dispatched to him that he should bring her merchandise. He dispatched to her: he has no need to bring merchandise to a buyer's house, even if she is an emperor's daughter; whoever needs merchandise should come to him. And no one can force a merchant into that, so the emperor's daughter decided to go to him. And her custom was: whenever she would go in the marketplace, she would veil

Sippurei Maasiyot – Chapter 10

her face in order that one should not gaze at her, for people would be liable to fall down and be left in weakness etc. due to her beauty. The emperor's daughter went, covering her face, and she took her ladies with her and a watch followed her. And she came to the merchant that is, to the murderer, who disguised himself as a merchant and she bought some wares from him and went her way. He told her that is, the murderer, the merchant, "If you come once more, I will show you even more beautiful articles than this, very wonderful things." And she returned home. After that, she came once again and bought merchandise from him and again went home. And the murderer stayed there for a while. Meanwhile, the emperor's daughter already became accustomed to visiting him; she would go to him often.

One day she came to him. He went and opened for her the room where the golden birds and so forth were located. She saw it being a very extraordinary novelty; and the other people who were with her that is, the watch, etc. also wanted to go into the room. He said, "No, no! I don't show this to anyone except you because you are the emperor's daughter, but for others, I don't want to show this at all." She alone entered in there, and he too went in the room, and he locked the door and did a crude thing and took a sack and forcefully put her in the sack. And he took off all her clothes from her and dressed a sailor in the clothing, veiled his face, pushed him out, and said to him, "Go!"

Sippurei Maasiyot – Chapter 10

And the sailor, not knowing whatsoever what's happening to him, as soon as he emerged with his face covered, the soldiers that is, the watch being unaware immediately began walking with him; they thought that this is the emperor's daughter. And the sailor went along with the troop wherever they led him; and not knowing whatsoever where in the world he is, he came there into the room where the emperor's daughter lived. His face was uncovered and they noticed that this is a plainly a sailor. There was a tremendous uproar there. And the sailor was slapped quite thoroughly in the face and was shoved out, since he is after all not responsible, for he didn't know at all.

And the murderer took the emperor's daughter, and he knew that he would certainly be chased after. He left the ship and hid together with her in a pit containing rainwater until the uproar would subside. And the ship's sailors he ordered to immediately cut anchors and flee right away, for they would certainly be pursued; and the ship would certainly not be shot at on account of the emperor's daughter, for they will think that she is there on the ship. "However, they will pursue you; therefore, you should flee immediately. If they catch you, so what?" - as the way of murderers is; they do not look at themselves at all in other words, they disregard themselves. And such is what happened; there was a big outcry and they were immediately chased; however, she was not found there. And the murderer hid together

Sippurei Maasiyot – Chapter 10

with her in a pit of rainwater, and they lay there. And he scared her so that she wouldn't scream, in order that people should not hear. And he said to her thus: "I have risked my life for your sake in order to capture you, and if I should lose you again, my life is not worth anything at all to me: for since you are already in my hand, if I should lose you again and you be taken away from me, then my life is already worth nothing to me. Therefore, as soon as you just give a yell I will strangle you right away, and let whatever happens to me happen, for I consider myself worthless in that case." She was terrified of him in other words, the emperor's daughter who was lying in the pit with the murderer was afraid to scream since the murderer had scared her.

Then he departed from there with her and he brought her to a city and they traveled on and traveled on, and they came to a place and the murderer understood that there too they are searching. He hid together with her in a mikveh. And then he went out from there too and came to another place, and they're also he hid with her in another water, and thus he hid with her each time in another water until he had hidden with her in all the seven kinds of waters that the burgher had hidden himself in with her mother, as mentioned, which constitute the seven witnesses, as mentioned until he came with her to the sea. The murderer searched there for even a small boat from which they catch fish, in order to cross with her. He found

Sippurei Maasiyot – Chapter 10

a ship; he took the emperor's daughter, and he did not need her, for he was a eunuch as mentioned, but just wanted to sell her to some king. And he had feared lest she is snatched away from him, so he went ahead and dressed her in sailor's clothes; she looked like a male. And the murderer traveled with her on the sea. [that is, with the emperor's daughter, whom we refer to in male terms, as the murderer disguised her thus, as mentioned. Because in this language our rabbi told us, his memory is a blessing, because the murderer dressed her as a male].

A storm wind came and carried away the ship to a shore, and the boat was broken and they came to the shore where the wilderness was, where the young man was living. When they came there, and the pirate was expert in routes, as usual, he knew that here it is desert; that no ships come here. Therefore, he no longer had any fear of any man and he let her loose. And they walked that is, the murderer and the emperor's daughter, he this way and she that way, to find themselves some bit of food. She distanced herself from the robber and the robber went his own way, and he noticed that she isn't here beside him. He began to shout out to her, and she made up her mind and did not respond to him at all, for she thought to herself, "My end is that he will sell me. Why should I answer him? If he reaches me again, I will reply to him I did not hear, especially as he does not want to kill me, for he wants to sell me." She

Sippurei Maasiyot – Chapter 10

did not respond to him and she went further on. And the robber sought her here and there and could not find her. And he went further and still could not find her; so probably vicious animals ate her up.

And she went further and further and was able to find some food, and walked on this until she came to the place where the young man was living that is, the aforementioned burgher's son. And by this time, she was now overgrown with hair, and in addition, she was dressed as a male in sailor's clothes as mentioned. They did not recognize one another. And immediately when she came, he turned very happy that another person had come here. He asked her, "Where have you come here from?" She answered, "I was with a merchant on the sea" etc. She asked him, "Where did you come here from?" He also answered her, "Through a merchant." The two of them remained there.

After the emperor's daughter was snatched away from the emperor, as mentioned, the empress lamented a great deal and struck her head on the wall over the loss of her daughter, and she ate away at the emperor with words a great deal and said to him, "Because of your pride you've wasted the young man, and now our daughter has become lost!" And she said to him, "She was our entire fortune and our entire success. Now we've lost her. What is left for me?" So, she ate away at him severely. And for himself as well this was certainly also very bitter that his daughter had become lost; in

Sippurei Maasiyot – Chapter 10

addition, the empress ate away at and infuriated him very much. So, there were severe quarrels and bickering between them, and she would say nasty things to him until she angered him very much until he ordered her banished. And he had judges sit trial on her; they ruled that she be banished, and she was banished. Afterward, the emperor was sent out into war and was not successful; he blamed this on some general: "Because you did so, therefore you lost the war." He banished the general. After that, he was sent off again into war and again was not successful. He banished more generals, and so he banished a number of generals. The country saw that he was doing bizarre things: first, he banished the empress, then the generals. They decided [that is, the citizens]: maybe the other way around - the empress should be sent for, he should be banished and she should lead the country. They did so and banished the emperor, and the empress they took back and she led the country. And the empress immediately sent for the burgher and his wife the **Burgheress** to be brought back as the emperor had brought them low and made them into paupers as mentioned, etc. And she brought them into her palace.

And the emperor, while he was being sent into exile, went ahead and begged those who were leading him that they should release him, "for, after all, I have been your emperor and must certainly have done good things for you. Now do this for me and let me go, for I will certainly not turn back to the country any longer. You

Sippurei Maasiyot – Chapter 10

need to have no fear. Release me. Let me go my way. Let me at least be free, the little bit of life that I have yet to live." They released him, and he went on and went on. Meanwhile, several years passed by and the emperor went on and went on until he reached the sea. The wind carried away his boat too and he too reached the aforementioned wilderness, until he came to the place where the other two were living that is, where the young man, the burgher's son, and his daughter the beauty who was now going dressed as a male, were. They did not recognize one another, for the emperor had already become overgrown with hair and already several years had passed, and they too had become overgrown with hair as mentioned. They asked him, "Where have you come here from?" He answered them, "Through a merchant." And they answered him thus as well. The three of them stayed there together, eating and drinking there, as mentioned. And they played on musical instruments there, for they all were able to play, for this one is an emperor and likewise they too were able to play.

And he, that is, the young man was the highly capable person among them, for he had been there since long ago already. And he would bring them meat, and they ate, and they would burn wood there, which was more precious than gold in settled places. The young man used to prove to them that here it is good for them to live out their years. According to the

Sippurei Maasiyot – Chapter 10

benefits that people have on earth in settled places, it is better that they should stay here, living out their worldly existence here. They asked him, "What sort of good did you have, that you say is better for you here?" He answered them and told them what had happened to him: how he had been a burgher's son etc. until he came here, and what his being a burgher's son resulted in for him. Here too he has all the good. Thus did the young man keeps saying to them. And he kept proving to them that here it is good to live out their worldly lives.

The emperor asked him, "Have you heard of the emperor?" He answered him: he had heard. He asked him about the beauty: whether he had heard of her. He answered him also: Yes. The young man began to talk angrily and said, "That murderer!" As one who gnashes his teeth at the other person, so did the young man talk angrily about the emperor of whom they were speaking, for he did not know that the emperor himself is talking with him. He asked him, "Why is he a murderer?" He answered him, "Because of his cruelty and because of his arrogance I've arrived here. He asked him, "How did that happen?" The young man made up his mind that here he has no need to fear anyone, so he spoke to him and recounted the entire story that happened to him. He asked him, "If the emperor should come into your hand would you take revenge on him now?" He answered him. No, for he was a good person

Sippurei Maasiyot – Chapter 10

and merciful "on the contrary, I would provide sustenance for him just as I sustain you." Again, the emperor began to sigh and groan, saying, "What an evil and bitter old age this emperor has!" For he had heard that his daughter the beauty had become lost, and he himself has been banished. Again, the young man spoke up, "Because of his cruelty in other words, mercilessness and because of his pride he squandered himself and his daughter and I have been cast off to here - all because of him." Again, he asked him the emperor to the young man, "If he should come into your hand would you take revenge on him?" He answers him, "No. I would sustain him precisely as I sustain you." The emperor made himself known to him and informed him that he himself is the emperor, and what has befallen him. The young man fell on him, kissed him, and hugged him. And she, that is, the beauty, who was also present, only in disguise, etc. was listening to everything as the two were talking to one another.

And the young man, it was his routine that he would go every day and make a sign for himself on three trees and look for the writing there that is, in these three of the trees. For there were millions of trees, so he would make himself a sign on those which he searched, in order that he should no longer need to search in these three trees tomorrow. Thus, he kept doing every day; perhaps he would still find the writing that is, the note she had sent him which

Sippurei Maasiyot – Chapter 10

he had lost among the trees, as mentioned. And when he would return from there he would come with wept-out eyes, for he would cry when he searched and could not find. They asked him that is, the emperor and the beauty asked him, "What do you look for among the trees and then come back with wept-out eyes?" He told them the entire story: insofar as the emperor's daughter that is, the beauty had sent him writing; he had hidden it in one of the trees; a storm wind came, etc. as mentioned. Now he searches; maybe he'll find it. They said to him, "Tomorrow when you go look, we will also go with you. Maybe we will find the note." And so it was; they went with him too. The emperor's daughter found the note in a tree, and she opened it up and saw this is her own writing from her hand. She reckoned if she immediately discloses to him that this is she herself, that if she will again remove these clothes and return again to her beauty and again be a good-looker as before, he may collapse and pass away. And she wants that it should be done in a kosher way, according to traditional practice in other words, she cannot marry him here in the wilderness, for she needs to have a wedding with him, as it ought to be. She went and returned the writing to him and told him that she had found the writing. In other words, she did not tell him that this is she herself; rather, she simply told him that she had found the writing. He immediately dropped down and was left faint. They restored him to health and

Sippurei Maasiyot – Chapter 10

there was great rejoicing among them.

Later the young man said, "What use is the writing for me? How will I ever be able to find her? For surely, she is now with some king for he thought that she had been sold by the murderer, just as the emperor had told him. What use is it for me? I will live out my years here." And he went and gave her back the writing and said to her, "Here! Take the note for yourself and you go and marry her" for she was disguised as a male. She allowed herself to go but asked him to go with her as well. "For I will certainly take her; things will be good for me; I'll give you a share of my good." In other words, the emperor's daughter who was disguised as a male said thus to the young man. And the young man saw that "he" is a wise man and will certainly take her; he was willing to go with him that is, with the emperor's daughter who he thought is a male. But the emperor was left alone, for he was afraid to go back to his country. She asked him to go too: for he will surely take the beauty. "You no longer have anything to fear. (In other words, she said to him, I will certainly seek out the beauty, so you no longer have anything to fear, for the **Mazal** will turn back when she is found. And you will also be ordered to return".

The three set out together and they hired a ship and came to the country where the empress lives, and they came to the city where she is located and they put the ship down. The emperor's daughter figured: if she immediately

Sippurei Maasiyot – Chapter 10

informs her mother that she has come back, she may pass away. She went and dispatched to her mother inasmuch as there is a man who has knowledge of her daughter. Then she herself went to the empress and told her what had happened to her daughter, telling her the entire story. And at the end she said to him in these terms, "And she that is, the daughter is also here." She told her the truth: "I myself am she!" And she informed her that her groom, that is, the burgher's son, is here too; however, she said to her mother that she wants it no other way except that her father the emperor be restored to his place. However, her mother did not want this at all, for she was very upset at him, because all this was due to him, but nonetheless she had to do it for the sake of her daughter. They wanted to bring him back the emperor; they searched for the emperor - and he's not there at all. Her daughter told out her that the emperor is also here with her. The wedding took place; the joy was entire. And the kingdom and the empire they took over, that is, the burgher's son with the beauty who got married; and they reigned over the face of the earth, that is, they reigned over the entire world.

Afterwards as well the old emperor had no greatness, for it the trouble, was all because of him. The burgher had enormous greatness - he is the emperor's father, who is the essential one **Ikar** [the root]. The sailor was smacked and smacked in the face and expelled.

Sippurei Maasiyot – Chapter 10

Regarding Lot it says – **Ha'hárah himmalét** [To the mountain flee for salvation] this is a burgher, and from him comes and born **Mashiach**. That will come soon in our day, Amen.

Jews had, in Mitzrayim, signs who would be the Redeemer, etc. - **Paqódh Paqádh'ti** [I have remember-remembered you] alternately, a chief I have appointed? - he who says to them these terms are the Redeemer. And it is an astounding thing since all Yisrael knew of this - so then what is this sign? Possibly it was not transmitted except to the elders. And upon the final Redeemer, there are certainly signs as well.

Mashiach will say to every Jew everything that has happened to him every single day, Tamar also lost the signs, as it says in the Midrash. Also, when she was going to be burned the **S"M** [The angel of death] came and removed the signs from her, and the angel Gabriel came and returned them, as it says in Midrash; out from her comes Mashiach, speedily in our days, Amen.

All this the Rebbe discussed after the story so that one can make some kind of surmise how far the story reaches. So, good for one who is privileged to know the stories' secret even in the other world!

Regarding that which is explained in the story, that everyone comes with his song of desire and some are replied to via an emissary etc. as mentioned - so there are a number of great

Sippurei Maasiyot – Chapter 10

people who each do what they do [And each says songs and so forth] and each busies himself and wants to reach - except the one who is worthy **re'ui** [eligible] for it. And some are answered via an emissary, or from under [behind] the wall or they show them the face etc. as in the story. However, in the end, when they leave this world, they answer them that they've still done nothing at all, like it is written in the story, how the beauty ultimately answers them, until the right leader comes - speedily in our days, Amen! This to the Rebbe z"l discussed.

Sippurei Maasiyot – Chapter 11

Chapter 11

The King's Son and Bondmaid's Son Who Were Switched

There once was a king. In his home there was a **Shifchah** [bondmaid] who served the queen. Generally, no cook may enter in the king's presence, but this bondmaid had some other service, a minor service. The time came when the queen was supposed to have a child, and the bondmaid had to give birth at that time as well. The **Meyaledeth** [midwife] went and switched the babies to see what will happen; what will arise from this. So, she took the king's child and put him down next to the bondmaid, and the bondmaid's son she put by the queen.

Afterwards the children began to grow up, and the king's son that is, the child who grew up at the king's whom they thought was the king's son, they promoted that is, made great and kept raising higher and higher until he became extremely great and was a very important person. And the bondmaid's son that is, he who was reared by the bondmaid, who in truth was the king's son also grew up at the maids, and both children studied together in one schoolroom. And the king's true son who shall be called "the bondmaid's son", his nature was drawn to the manners of royalty, except that he was brought up in the home of the servant. Conversely, the bondmaid's son, who shall be called **the king's son**, his nature was drawn to a different deportment not like the bearing of a king is, except that he was brought up in the king's home so he had to act according to the manners of a royal person, because those were the manners, they brought him up with.

Now the granny, because women are **Da'athan kaloth** [light minded], in other words, they cannot hold themselves back, went and spoke out the secret to some person, inasmuch as she had exchanged the children. Now, every person has a friend, and that friend has another friend, thus one person told the other until the secret was revealed, as the way of the world is, until the world was talking quietly about it, that the king's son was switched. But it was not permitted to speak about it outright, so that the king should not become aware of it, for what will the king be able to do in such a case, since he cannot correct it? For he cannot believe it, as perhaps it is a lie, so how can one reverse the exchange? Therefore, one certainly may not say it out in front of the king; however, amongst themselves the public talked about it quietly.

The day arrived when someone came along and told out the secret before the king's son, inasmuch as they say about him that he was exchanged. "However, you cannot investigate this, for it does not befit you. And how can one probe such a thing? Just, I am telling it to you in order that you should know. For perhaps there will once be a conspiracy against the monarchy; the conspiracy will be able to prevail through this, for they will say that they are taking to themselves the king's son as a king, that is, the one who they say of him that he is the king's true son, as mentioned before. Therefore, you need to outwit the fellow." [All this said that person to the king's son who in actual truth is the bondmaid's son, as mentioned].

The king's son [that is, the one who is called the king's son. And the rule is that wherever simply "the king's son" is mentioned, it refers to the exchanged one. That is, he is actually the bondmaid's son, except that he is called the king's son because he was raised at the kings. And similarly, with the **bondmaid's son** where a bondmaid's son is mentioned: only where "the king's true son" or "the bondmaid's true son" is mentioned, then the meaning is the actual truth]. went and began to do mischief to the other one's father [who was really his own father], and arranged everything to constantly do him evil. And he kept dealing him mischiefs one after another in order that he should have to be uprooted.

Afterwards the king grew old and died, so he assumed the **Reign** [the bondmaids's son who is now called the king's son, as mentioned above]; then he dealt even more evil to the other son's father [to the father of the bondmaid's son who in truth was the king's son; and this father was really his own father, of the one who had taken up the reign, for they were exchanged, as above]. And he dealt him evil disguised so that people would not know that it's from him, for it's unseemly in front of people, and kept dealing him mischiefs one after another.

This one the son's father understood that he is dealing him woes on account of the matter that is, because the public discusses that the children were exchanged. He that is, the bondservant, the bondmaid's husband who was constantly dealt woes in order that he should drive out his son because they say that the children were exchanged, as mentioned spoke up and said to his son and told him the whole affair and said to him, "I have great pity on you, for any way you approach it **Mimah Nafshakh** [from wherever your soul is drawn]," possibly a double meaning here - if indeed you are my child, of course I certainly have great pity on you; if indeed you are not my child but are in truth the king's son, there is even greater pity on you, because that one that is, he who took over the reign wants to expel you entirely, perish the thought. Therefore, you must pull up that is, run away from here." It irritated him very much and he felt very bad about the thing. However, the king that is, the one who became king in place of his father, because it seemed he is the king's son due to the interchange meanwhile kept constantly dealing out woes one after another, so the son that is, the king's true son who was exchanged decided he must run away. His father gave him a great deal of

Sippurei Maasiyot – Chapter 11

money and he left. It upset him very much that he was driven out of his country for nothing, for he looked around him: "Why do I deserve it that I should be driven out? If indeed I am the king's son, I certainly don't deserve this, that I should be driven out. And even if I am not the king's son, I also don't deserve this, that I should be a fugitive that is, one who has run away for nothing. For, what is my sin? What am I guilty of here?" It upset him very much, and on account of this he took to the drink and went to brothels that is, to houses where there are whores. And with that he wanted to spend his years, getting drunk and following after what his heart desires, because he was driven away for nothing.

And the king that is, the false prince, the exchanged one who became king took over the kingship strongly, and when he heard anything about people murmuring and discussing anything about it that is, that they were switched, as mentioned he penalized them in other words, punished and tortured and took his revenge on them. So, he ruled with force and strength .

And the day came to pass when the king went with his noblemen on a **Na Ulavi** [Catch] that is, catching animals and they came to a pleasant place. And a river of water was ahead of that spot, so they stopped there to rest themselves and they wanted to walk around. The king lay down for a little bit, and the deed that he had done, that he had driven away that certain

Sippurei Maasiyot – Chapter 11

person for nothing, came to his mind. For, any way you look at it: if he's indeed the king's son, is it not enough that he was exchanged? Why should he in addition be driven out for nothing? And if he is not the king's son, he also does not deserve to be driven away, for what had he done wrong? The king thought himself away in this matter, and had remorse over the transgression and the great injustice that he had done. And the king could give himself no advice what he should do here. And to talk about it - one cannot do such a thing with any person at all, to take counsel with him for one is obviously ashamed to discuss such things with people. So, the king became very laden with great worry. He ordered the nobles to turn back, because since worry has befallen him there is no need to tour any more. They returned home. When the king returned home, he of course had numerous affairs and concerns, and he busied himself with his concerns and the thing left his mind that is, the worry and the remorse that he had over the fact that he had driven away the other for no reason. **And** the one who was driven away that is, the king's true son - well, he did what he did and squandered his money. One time, he went out alone for a walk; and he lay down and it came to his mind what had happened to him and he thought: "What has God done to me? If I am indeed the king's son, I certainly don't deserve this, and if I am not the king's son, I also don't deserve this selfsame thing, that I

Sippurei Maasiyot – Chapter 11

should be a fugitive and an exile." Then he reached Locality in his mind, "Just the reverse. If it is so, that Hashem Blessed is He, can indeed do such a thing, that they should exchange a king's son and such things should befall him - do I turn myself to behave this way? Is it right, what I have done? Does it befit me that I should behave thus, the way I have done?" And he began to have great anguish and very much regret the bad deeds he had done. Then he turned back home, there where he was staying, and further took to the drink. However, because he had already begun to have remorse, the thoughts of remorse and repentance which came to his mind all the time would confuse him. One time he laid himself down to sleep and the dream came to him to the effect: In such and such a place there is a fair on such and such a day; therefore, he should go there, and whatever he strikes first - any gainful service - he should immediately do it, even if it won't be according to his dignity thus went his dream. And he woke up with a start and the dream was very much in his thought. For sometimes it happens that the matter immediately goes out from the thought. But rather, this dream very much entered in his thought. Albeit, nonetheless, it seemed very hard for him to do this, and he went more to the drink. And the dream appeared to him again several times, and the dream confused him a great deal.

One time they said to him in the dream, "If you want to have pity on yourself, do thus" that is,

Sippurei Maasiyot – Chapter 11

he should go to the fair etc. as mentioned, so now he had to carry out the dream. And he went ahead and left the remaining money he still had, leaving it at the inn where he was staying; and the good clothes which he had, he also left at the inn; and he took for himself a simple garment like merchants, that is, a coverall, and he set out for the fair and arrived there. And he got up very early and went to the fair.

A certain merchant encountered him and said to him, "Would you like to earn something?" He answered him, "Yes." He said to him, "I need to drive herds behemoth, dumb beasts here. Will you hire yourself out to me?" And he didn't have time to settle his mind, due to the dream for the dream had been that he must take on the first gainful work etc. as mentioned, and he immediately answered - **Yes**. And the merchant immediately hired him and immediately began to lord over him like a master over his servants. And he began to look around himself, what he had done, for he certainly doesn't deserve such a servitude, for he is a delicate man and now he'll have to drive herds and go by foot next to the beasts. However, one already can't have any regret, and the merchant is lording over him like a master. He asked the merchant, "How shall I go alone with the herds?" He answered, "I have more herdsmen driving my herds. You'll go together with them," and he gave over to his hands certain herds to drive. He led the herds out of the town, and there, gathered together, were the rest of the herdsmen driving beasts. They went together; he was driving the herds, and the merchant was riding on a horse and going along with them. And the merchant was driving cruelly that is, with anger and without compassion, and against him he was extra cruel, and he grew more and more terrified of the merchant, since he saw in him that he has extremely great cruelty and anger against him. And he feared in case he deals him a blow with his stick then he'll die instantly for the king's true son was quite a frail person and on account of his sensitivity he was very terrified, thus he thought that way. So, he was walking with the herds, and the merchant with them. And they came to a certain spot; they took the sack wherein lies the herdsmen's bread, and he the merchant gave them to eat; him too they gave from the bread and he ate.

Afterwards, they were walking by a very thick forest; two beasts from his herds of this son who had become a herder for the merchant walked off into the forest. The merchant yelled at him and he went after the beasts to capture them. And the beasts ran away further and he pursued them more; and since the forest was very thick, it was as soon as he entered the forest that they already could not see each other, so he immediately disappeared that is, became hidden from their eyes that is, from the rest who were going with him. And he that is, the king's true son from whom the two beasts walked off, kept going and still chasing after

Sippurei Maasiyot – Chapter 11

the beasts and they kept running away. And he chased after them a great deal, until he arrived in the thick of the forest.

He made up his mind - Either way [be what will be], I'm already going to die, because if I return without the beasts I'll die through the merchant" for on account of the great fear that he had of the merchant, it seemed to him that the merchant would kill him if he returns without the beasts. And if I'll be here, I will also die by the animals of the forest." He decided, "Why should I return to the merchant? How can I come to him without the beasts?" For he had great fear of him. He went and chased further after the beasts and they kept running away. Meanwhile it became night, and such a thing he has never had, that he should have to sleep alone at night in such a thick forest. And he heard the roaring of the beasts which roared in their usual way. He made up his mind and went up on a tree and spent the night there, and he heard the sound of the beasts yelling in their usual way.

In the morning he took a look: he saw that the beasts are standing close by him. He got down the tree and went to catch them; they got away further. He went after them more and they got away more. And the beasts found themselves some grasses to eat there and they stopped to graze. He went further to catch them; they got away further. And thus, he kept going after them and they run away, he goes after them more and they run away - until he has arrived

Sippurei Maasiyot – Chapter 11

in very thick forest where there were already animals that have no fear whatsoever of any people, because they are far from settled places. And again, it has become night and he heard the sound of the animals roaring and he was very terrified. Meanwhile he noticed that a very large tree is standing there, and he got up on the tree. As soon as he was up on the tree he noticed: a man is lying there. He took fright but still he was relieved for the reason that he has found a human here. They asked one another, "Who are you?" "A man." "Who are you?" "A man." "From where have you come here?" He did not want to tell what had happened to him, so he answered him, "By way of the dumb beasts which I tended. Two beasts walked off here, and thereby I've arrived here." In return he asked the other man whom he found there on the tree, "From where did you get here?" He answered him, "I got here by the horse. For I was riding on a horse; I stopped to take a rest and the horse went off into the forest. I chased after it to catch it and the horse ran away further, until I arrived here".

They made up between them that they should remain together, and they agreed that even when they will come into civilization they should also remain together. And the two of them slept the night there and they heard the sound of the beasts roaring and screaming very much. Towards day he heard a **Kha-Kha-Kha** [Very great laughter] over the entire forest in other words, the sound of the laughter went

Sippurei Maasiyot – Chapter 11

over all the forest, for it was a very great laughter, to the extent that the tree trembled from the sound of the laughter, and he became very terrified and had great fear from it. The other person said to him that is, the man whom he had found there on the tree, "I already have no fear of it whatsoever, for I've slept here already several nights. All nights are like this; as it gets close to day, one hears the laughter, to the extent that all the trees tremble and quake".

He was very frightened and said to the other, "It seems that here is the place of **Those People** [the demons], for in settled areas one does not hear such a laughter at all, for who has heard a laughter over the entire world?" Then immediately it became day. They took a look; they saw: the beasts of his are standing, and the horse of the other is also standing. They went down and started chasing after - this one after the beasts and that one after the horse. And the beasts ran away further, and he chases more, etc. as before. And likewise, the other keeps chasing after the horse and the horse keeps running away until they [the two men] have gone off, one from the other, and one already did not know of the other's whereabouts.

Meanwhile, the king's son who was still chasing after the beasts found a sack with bread. Now, this is certainly very important in a wilderness, so he took the sack on his shoulders and went after the beasts. Meanwhile, he encountered a man. Initially, he

Sippurei Maasiyot – Chapter 11

was afraid; however, still he had a little relief because has he found a person here. The man asked him, "How did you get here?" He asked the other man in return, "How did you get here?" The other man answered him, "I with an expression of amazement - my parents and my parents' parents were raised here. But you, how have you come here? For, no man whatsoever comes here from the settled areas." He was very frightened, for he understood that this is no human being at all, for he says his ancestors were raised here and no man from civilization comes at all here, so he understood that this is no human at all. But still, he did not do anything to him whatsoever and was welcoming that is, this man of the forest did not do any harm to the king's true son who was going after the beasts.

And the man of the forest said to him, "What are you doing here?" He answered: he is chasing after the dumb beasts. The man of the forest said to him, "Stop chasing after your sins already, for it is not beasts at all but rather your sins are leading you around like this. Enough already! You have already received yours that is, your punishment you've already received. Now stop chasing them anymore. Come with me; you will arrive at the thing that is fitting for you." He went with him, and he was afraid to speak with him and to ask him anything, for a man like this may open up his mouth and swallow him down. He followed him.

Sippurei Maasiyot – Chapter 11

Meanwhile, he encountered his friend who was chasing after the horse. As soon as he saw him, he immediately winked at him to signal that "this is no human being at all; don't have any dealings with him whatsoever, because this is not at all a human." And he immediately went and whispered it to him in his ear, that this is not a human being at all, etc. Meanwhile, his friend that is, the horseman took a look and he saw: he has a sack with bread on his shoulder! He began to appeal to him, "My brother! It is already days that I have not eaten. Give me bread!" He answered him, "Here in the wilderness nothing helps, for my life takes priority; I need the bread for my sake." He began to beg him and beseech him greatly, "I'll give what I'll give you!" Except, in the wilderness certainly no gift helps at all for bread." He answered him, "What can you give me for bread in the wilderness?" He said to him that is, the horseman who begged for the bread said to the herdsman, who is the king's true son, "I give away myself entirely; I will sell myself to you as a servant for the bread." That is, the herdsman decided: "To purchase a man it's worth it to give him bread," and he bought him as a permanent slave. And he swore him in with oaths that he shall be a slave to him forever, even when they arrive in civilization, and he will give him bread, that is, they shall both eat from the sack of bread until it runs out.

And the both of them went together and followed the man of the forest, and the slave

Sippurei Maasiyot – Chapter 11

walked behind him that is, the horseman who sold himself as a slave followed after the herdsman, for he was already his slave, and the two of them walked after the man of the forest. And meanwhile, now it became a little bit easier for him, since he has a servant already. When he needed to lift up some object or do something else, he ordered his slave to lift it or do something. So, they followed together behind the man of the forest and they came to a place where there were snakes and scorpions; he grew very terrified, and on account of fear he asked the man of the forest, "How will we get past here?" He answered him, "**Ella ma'i** [but what then] - how will you enter my house?" - and showed him his house standing in the air. They went with him and he brought them over in peace, and he brought them into his house, gave them things to eat and to drink, and went away.

And the king's true son who had driven the beasts ordered his slave around for whatever he needed. It upset the slave very much that he had sold himself as a slave for the sake of a single hour when he needed bread to eat because now, he already has what to eat and just for the sake of a single hour he will be an eternal slave. And he made a big sigh and groaned, "What have I come to, that I should be a slave?" He asked him that is, the king's true son, who was his master, asked him, "What kind of greatness did you have, that you sigh that you have come to this?" He answered him and recounted to him

Sippurei Maasiyot – Chapter 11

to the effect: He had been a king; they said about him that he had been exchanged etc., as above for this horseman was really the king himself, who was actually the bondmaid's son; he drove his friend away that is, the king's true son. One time it came to his mind that he has done not right and he regretted etc. Regrets kept coming to him constantly over the evil deed and over the great injustice that he has done against his friend. Once, the dream appeared to him that his correction is that he should throw away the kingship and go wherever his eyes will bring him, and by this, he will rectify his error. He didn't want to do it, but those same dreams kept perplexing him constantly, that he should do so until it remained in his mind that he should do so. So, he threw away the kingship and went where he went until he came here. And now he'll be a slave. Now the other one hears all this and keeps silent that is, the king's true son who had driven beasts heard out all this that he told him, and he thought to himself, "I will know well enough how to deal with you".

At night, the man of the forest came and gave them to eat and to drink, and they spent the night there. Towards day they heard the great laughter mentioned earlier until all the trees trembled; it broke all the trees, the sound of the laughter. He urged him that is, the slave urged the king's true son, who is his master, to ask the man of the forest what it is. He asked him, "What is this such great laughter, close today?"

Sippurei Maasiyot – Chapter 11

He answered him, "This is the day laughing at the night, for the night asks the day, 'Why when you come do I have no name?' The day lets out a big laugh and then it becomes day. And this is the laughter that is heard close today." This was a big wonder to him, for this is something extraordinary, that the day laughs at the night. He could already ask no more when the other answers with such language. In the morning again the man of the forest went away and they ate and drank there; at night he came back and they ate and drank and spent the night there. At night they heard the sound of the animals as they all screamed and roared with wild sounds. The lion screamed, the leopard roared with another sound, and similarly the rest of the beasts, each beast roaring with a different sound, and the birds whistled and clicked, and so all gave voice with wild sounds. And at the beginning they became very scared; they did not listen correctly to the sound on account of fear. Later, they bowed their ears and listened; they heard it's a sound of a melody; they sing quite a nice tune which is an extraordinary novelty. They listened even more; they heard it's an extraordinarily fine melody that is quite a wild marvel which was an extremely great pleasure to hear, [such] that all the pleasures of the world are completely nothing and amount to absolutely nothing in comparison to the wildly great pleasure that one has when one hears this wondrous tune. They discussed between themselves that they want already to

Sippurei Maasiyot – Chapter 11

remain here, since for eating and drinking they have, and they have such a delight that is such a marvel that all kinds of delights of the world were entirely nullified against this pleasure. The slave urged his master that is, the king's true son to ask him that is, the man of the forest what it is; he asked him.

He answered him: Inasmuch as the sun has made a garment for the moon, all the animals of the forest have spoken up to the effect that the moon does them great favors, for the animals' dominion is mainly at night only. For sometimes they need to go into a settled area, and by day they cannot, so of course, the main time of their dominion is only at night. And the moon does them such a favor by shining for them at night; therefore, they agreed that they should make a new melody in honor of the moon, and this is the tune that you hear. When they heard it's a melody they listened even more; they heard it's quite a lovely, sweet melody that is an extremely wild novelty.

He replied to them that is, the man of the forest "What - is this such a novelty for you? **Ella ma'i** [But what then?] - I have an instrument which I've received from my forebears, who inherited it from their forebears' forebears, which this instrument was made with such things, with such leaves, and with such colors, that when one takes the instrument and puts it on whatever beast or on whatever bird then it immediately begins to play this melody that is, the melody that the animals played." Then the

Sippurei Maasiyot – Chapter 11

laughter happened again and it became day; the man of the forest again went away and he that is, the king's true son went searching for the instrument. And he searched out the entire room and did not find it, and he was fearful to go any further. And they that is, the king's true son with his slave who is the bondmaid's son who before was king were afraid to say to the man of the forest that he should lead them into the settlement. Later the man of the forest came and said to them that he would lead them into the settlement. He led them into the settlement, and he took the instrument and gave it to the king's true son and said to him, "The instrument I give to you. And with him that is, with his slave who before was king, etc. - you will know how to deal with him." They asked him, "Where shall we go?" He said to them that they should inquire after the land that is called by this name: "The Foolish Land with the Wise King." They asked him, "To which **Tzad** [side] should we start to ask after this land?" He showed them with his hand: right here as someone points with a finger. The man of the forest said to the king's true son, "Go there, to the land, and there you will come to your greatness".

They went where they went, and they very much wished to find any animal or beast to test the instrument, whether it would be able to play as before. However, they still did not see any sort of animal. Then they arrived further into the settlement. They found some beast and laid the instrument down on it and it began to play the tune as before. So, they went and went until they came to the land. And the land was walled about and one could not enter in the land except by one gateway. One must go around several miles until one comes to the gateway. They went around until they came to the gateway. When they had now arrived at the gateway, they did not want to let them enter, inasmuch as the king of the land had died; the king's son remained and the king had left a will: "The Foolish Land with the Wise King", now it will already be called the reverse: "The Wise Land with the Foolish King". And whoever will undertake that he should return the land to the first name, that is, that they will once again call the land by its first name, "The Wise Land with the Foolish King". the same shall become king therefore, they do not let any man into the land except he who will undertake the same, that he should return the land to the first name. They said to him, "Can you undertake this, that you should return the country to its first name?" He certainly could not undertake this, so they could not enter. His slave urged him that they should return home. However, he did not want to return because the man of the forest had said to him that he should go to this land and there he will arrive at his greatness.

Meanwhile, another man arrived who was riding on a horse, and he wanted to go in but they also did not let him in on account of this as mentioned. Meanwhile, he noticed that this

Sippurei Maasiyot – Chapter 11

other man's horse is standing so he went ahead and took the instrument and laid it down on the horse and it began to play the very fine melody as above. The horseman pleaded with him very much that he should sell it to him, and he replied, "What can you give me for such a wondrous instrument"?

The horseman said to him, "Well, what can you do with this instrument except perform theatrics and take in a gulden? I however know a thing that is better than your instrument. I know a thing I've received from my parents' parents: to be an **Extrapolater**. That is, I know such a thing that I've received from the forebears of my forebears, that through this thing one can make an inference. When somebody says just any utterance, one knows, through that which I have received, one should discern something from one thing that is, one thing from the other. And I have not yet spoken out the thing before any man in the world. Therefore, I will teach out to you this certain thing, and you will give me this here instrument for that".

He decided that is, the king's true son, who had the instrument it is truly a great wonder to be an extrapolater. So, he gave away the instrument to him and he that is, the horseman went ahead and instructed him so that he should be an extrapolater. Now the king's true son, since he has now gotten the ability to extrapolate, was walking around there by the gate of the country, and he understood that it is

Sippurei Maasiyot – Chapter 11

indeed possible for him to undertake it to return the land to its first name. For he had now after all become an extrapolater; thus, he understood it is possible, even though he did not yet know just how and by what way he will be able to do this, to restore the first name to the country. But nevertheless, because he had become able to extrapolate, he understood it is possible. He made up his mind he would order himself let in and he would undertake it that he would return its first name to the country. What would he lose here? He said to those people who did not want to let him in that they should let him in and he will take under himself that very thing, that he would return the first name to the country. They let him in, and they informed the noblemen that there is found a man who wants to undertake it to return the land to the first name. They brought him to the noblemen of the land.

The noblemen said to him, "You should know that we too are no fools, God forbid, except the king that had been - he was a very extraordinarily great sage, such that against him we were all fools. Therefore, the land used to be called 'The Foolish Land with the Wise **Malkhuth** [Government]. Then the king died; the king's son remained, and the king's son is also a wise man, except against us he is not at all smart. Therefore, the land is now called conversely: The Smart Land with the Foolish Government. "The king left a will: when there will be found such a wise person that he should

Sippurei Maasiyot – Chapter 11

return the land to the first name, he shall be king. And he commanded his son that when such a man will be found, he shall step down from the reign for him: that is, when there will be found such a wise man that he will be such an extraordinarily great sage that against him everyone will be fooled, he will become king, for this man will surely bring back the land once more to its first name, The Foolish Land with the Smart King, for they are after all fools against him. Therefore, you should know what you are taking under yourself here." All such did the noblemen say to him.

In addition, they the noblemen again; this is all a continuation of their words, said to him, "The test will be whether you are this wise: Inasmuch as there is a garden that is leftover from a king who had been, who was a very great sage, and the garden is quite an extraordinary novelty - metal instruments grow in it [that is, tools of **ironwork**], silver instruments and gold instruments - so it is an extremely wild novelty: However, one cannot go in the garden, for when a person goes in the garden then immediately they begin chasing him. So, they chase and he screams and he doesn't at all know and doesn't at all see who is chasing him, and so they chase him continuously until they make him run away from the garden. Therefore, we shall see whether you are wise; if you'll be able to go into the garden." He asked whether they beat the person who enters. They said to him:

Sippurei Maasiyot – Chapter 11

the main thing is they chase him and he doesn't at all know who they are that chase him and he has to run away in very great panic. For thus people who had gone in there told them. All thus did the noblemen say to the king's true son.

He got up and went to the garden. He saw there is a wall around it, and the gate is open and there aren't any guards there, for one certainly doesn't need any guards for this garden, for no one is able to go in it, as mentioned! That is, the king's true son was walking by the garden and he took a look: he noticed that standing there by the garden is a man. That is, a man was portrayed there.

He understood because he had already gotten the ability to extrapolate, that it all depends on this man. When one enters the garden and they start to chase him, he needs not run away at all but just put himself next to the man; thereby he will be saved. Moreover, even if one takes this man and inserts him inside the interior of the garden then every man will be able to enter in peace into this garden. All this the king's true son understood because he had become able to infer. He got up and went inside the garden, and as soon as they started chasing him, he went and put himself next to the man standing by the garden from the outside, and thereby he emerged in peace and it did not harm him at all. For, others when they entered the garden and they started chasing them would run away in very great panic and be consequently battered,

Sippurei Maasiyot – Chapter 11

but he emerged in peace and tranquility by placing himself next to the man.

And the noblemen saw this and were astonished that he got out safely. Then he ordered that is, the king's true son call that they should take the man and insert him inside within the midst of the garden. They did so and then all the noblemen entered inside the garden and they passed through and got out safely.

The noblemen spoke up to him, "Still, even though we have seen from you such a thing, nevertheless for the sake of one thing you do not yet deserve to be given the kingship. We will try you further with one thing. Inasmuch as there is a throne here from the king who was, and the throne is very high and by the throne stand all sorts of animals and birds carved out of wood: And in front of the throne stands a little bed, and by the bed stands a table, and on the table stands a lamp. And from the throne emerge paved roads and the roads are walled and the roads go out from the throne to all **Zaytin** [sides]; see above where it is spelled with a tzaddi, and no man knows whatsoever what it is, the matter of the throne with these roads. And these roads, when they go out and extend for some distance, a golden lion is standing there. And if some man should go to it, it will open its mouth and swallow him down. And beyond this lion, the road extends even further, and likewise with the rest of the roads that go out from the throne. That is, with another road that goes out from the throne to another side it is also like that: when the road extends away from a piece, a different animal is standing there, namely a **lavi' lion** [leopard] of ironwork. And there too one cannot go to it as before, because it will swallow him down. And beyond the leopard the road extends further, and so it is with the rest of the roads. And these selfsame roads extend and go throughout the entire land, and no man whatsoever knows what is the thing of the throne with all these things and the roads. Therefore, you shall be tested with this, whether you will be able to know the matter of the throne with all these things".

They showed him the throne and he saw that it was very high, etc. He went to the throne, took a look, and understood that the throne was made of the little box's wood that is, the instrument that the man of the forest had given him. He looked some more and he saw the throne is lacking some little rose at the top **Shoshanah** [Rayzile], and if the throne would have this rose the throne would have the power of the little box, that is, the aforementioned instrument which had the power that when one would lay the instrument on some beast or animal it began to play, as mentioned. He looked some more and he saw that this rose which is missing at the top of the throne, rose is lying at the bottom in the throne. One needs to take the little rose out from below and seat it above and thus the throne will have the power of the little box. For the king who had been had

Sippurei Maasiyot – Chapter 11

done everything with wisdom and had disguised everything in order that no one should understand the matter - what it means - until there would come such an extraordinarily great sage who would surmise and would be able to hit upon interchanging everything and arranging all the things as needed.

And so, to the little bed: he understood that one needs to move it a bit away and back from the place where it's standing. And also, the table: one also needs to move it a bit away and back from [its] place, and one also needs the lamp a bit away and back from its place. And so, to the birds and animals: one also needs to relocate them all; one should take this bird from this place and put it on that place. And thus, with everything; one must reposition everything. For the king had purposely disguised everything cleverly in order that no one should know what is meant until there would come the wise man who would be able to understand he should arrange everything properly. And so, to the lion that stands there, where that road goes out: one needs to put it yonder. And likewise, all of them; one needs to relocate all of them. He ordered that they should arrange everything as needed: they should take out the little rose from below and seat it above, and likewise all the things - they should reposition all things and arrange them differently as needed; in the way he called for.

As soon as they did so, they all began playing the exquisite melody that is quite a wild novelty, and they all did what they needed to do. So, they gave him the kingship. that is the true king's son who demonstrated all the clever things, as above. He spoke up and said to the [actual] bondmaid's son: "Now I understand that I am indeed the real son of the king and you are really the bondmaid's son".

These too are the words of Rabbeinu **Nero Ya'ir**, [let his light shine], after he told this story he spoke up and said these words:

In former generations when they would discuss kabbalah it would be talked about in such language, as this story is: For until Rashb"i they would not discuss kabbalah openly; only Rashb"i disclosed kabbalah openly; and before when the friends would speak kabbalah they would speak in such language: "When they placed the ark upon the oxen they began singing." Now understand this.

For there are new states of the Moon when the moon receives innovations from the sun, and this is the aspect of when they bring the **Ark** to **Beith Shemesh** [City in Israel], and then all the creatures bearing the Throne make a new melody, the aspect of A Song: Sing to Hashem a new song," which is the song that the cows of Bashan sang. And this is the aspect of the bed, table, chair, and lamp; they are the restoration of the Shekhinah. And the aspect of the garden: for **Adam HaRishon** [Adam husband of Chava] was driven out of the Garden, and Shabbath guarded over him, as is brought in the books of kabbalah. And Shabbath is the aspect

Sippurei Maasiyot – Chapter 11

of "the king unto whom peace belongs," the aspect of the aforementioned man, who is the king during whose days there was peace, and therefore he stationed himself by Shabbath. And the rest he did not explain.

He spoke up and said after telling this story, in these words: This story is a big wonder, and it's entirely one: the herds, etc., the throne, etc. and the garden; it's all one. At times it is the aspect hinted to in the story is called by this name, at times by this name, all according to the **Inyan** [interest] and the aspect. And the things are very, very deep, wondrous, and awesome. [These two are the words of Rabbeinu let his light shine] And there is more, but there is no need to reveal everything. There is also that the king that was in that land did something corresponding to the sun and something corresponding to the moon that is, that these things alluded to the sun and the moon, and the moon was holding a lamp in its hand, and when the day arrives then the lamp does not shine, for **Shraga Betihara** [a Candle at midday day], etc. And this is that the night said to the day, "Why is it that when you arrive, I have no name?" [as expressed above], for in the day a lamp does not avail whatsoever.

The explanation of the story is like the throne which the king made, as mentioned, as the main wisdom is that one needs to know how to order the things; therefore whoever is adept in the books and his heart is whole can understand the explanation; however, the things have to be

Sippurei Maasiyot – Chapter 11

ordered well, for sometimes it is called this and sometimes it is called that, and likewise with the rest of the things, that is, with the explanation of the story, sometimes the man of the above story is called by this name, and sometimes by a different name, and similarly with the rest of the things. Fortunate is he who will be privileged to understand these things to their truth. All this he himself said after the story. Blessed be Hashem forever, Amen and Amen.

These are entirely Rabbeinu **haKadosh's** [The holy] words Z"L.

Chapter 12

The Prayer Meister

Once, there was a **Ba`al Tefilah** [Master of prayer, is the leader of a prayer service] who was constantly occupied only with prayer, songs and praises to the Blessed God. He dwelled outside of the **Yeshuv** [settled areas], and would regularly go into them to enter into - conversation with some person - typically people of lower stature, such as poor people, etc. He would speak to his heart about the purpose of the whole world, that truthfully there is no purpose other than being occupied with serving God every day of one's life, spending the days in prayer to Hashem Blessed his name, with songs and praises, etc. The Prayer Meister would speak with him at great length such words of spiritual arousal until they would enter his ears and the person would want to join him. As soon as the person would feel this desire to join, he would immediately take him and bring him to his dwelling place removed from civilization. For that **Ba'al Tefilah** had chosen for himself, as above, a place outside of settled areas, and there was a river there in front of him, as well as trees and fruits there too, and they would eat of the fruits and he was not strict about clothes at all.

Thus did the Prayer Meister regularly venture

Sippurei Maasiyot – Chapter 12

into the settled areas to charm and persuade people to serve Hashem Blessed his name, to join in his way of being occupied with prayer, etc. Whoever took a liking to him [and his message], he would take them away and bring them to his place outside civilization. There they would occupy themselves only with prayers, songs and praises to Hashem Blessed his name, as well as confessionals, fasts, privations that is, torturing one's body and repentance, etc. The **Ba'al Tefilah** would give them compilations of compositions he had in matters of prayers, songs, praises, confessions, etc. and they would be involved with them constantly. Eventually, there would be found, among those people whom he had brought there, those who could now also draw people close to Hashem Blessed his name. He would then give permission to one of his people that he, too would go into settled areas to be occupied with matters as above, to draw people close to Hashem Blessed his name.

And so, the **Ba'al Tefilah** would constantly be occupied with this matter, every time drawing more people close to Hashem Blessed his name, taking them out of civilization, as mentioned, until an impression was made in the world and the thing began to be known. For suddenly people would disappear from the country--it was unknown where they were. Thus, it would happen that suddenly one's son was missing and so forth, unknown where they were. Gradually, it became known that there

Sippurei Maasiyot – Chapter 12

exists a Prayer Meister who goes and seduces people into serving Hashem Blessed his name. However, it was impossible to recognize or catch him, because this **Ba'al Tefilah** would conduct himself very craftily and would change and switch himself by each and every person with a different transfiguration. By this one he would seem like a poor man, by that one, like a trader, and by another as something else, etc. Furthermore, when the **Ba'al Tefilah** would come to talk to people, when he understood that he could not accomplish his intent with them, he would so spin them around with words that they could not at all detect his good motives--as if his aim was not at all about his mission to draw them close to Hashem Blessed his name. For [the way he spoke made] it impossible to realize his intent for this even though, in truth his whole objective in speaking to people was only this to draw people close to Hashem Blessed his name. For his whole preoccupation was only this. It was only when he understood that he was not influencing him that the **Ba'al Tefilah** would so spin, misguide and deceive him until he was completely unable to perceive his good intentions. The **Ba'al Tefilah** remained occupied with this motif until an impression and infamy was made in the world; and they longed to catch him, but it was impossible, as mentioned.

So, the aforementioned **Ba'al Tefilah**, with his people, dwelled outside of settled areas, as above, and were involved only with matters, as

Sippurei Maasiyot – Chapter 12

above, with prayer, songs and praises to Hashem Blessed his name, and confessions, fasts, afflictions and repentances. It was also in the Prayer Meister's purview that he could provide for each and every person that which he needed. If he understood about one of his people that, according to his level of brain, he needed to go dressed in **Gilden Geshtik** [gold-embroidered clothes] for serving Hashem Blessed his name, he supplied it for him. So too the opposite, when sometimes some rich person would draw close to him and he would take him out from settled areas, as above, he would understand that this rich person needed to go in tattered, wretched clothes, he would make him go dressed that way. Everything was according to [the fact] that he would know exactly the revisionary needs of each and every person and would supply him [correspondingly]. For these people whom the **Ba'al Tefilah** drew close to Hashem Blessed his name, a fast or extensive self-mortification was dearer than all the world's delights, for they had more delight from the substantial self-affliction or fast than from all the world's delights.

And the day came to pass that there was a country where there were enormous riches, such that everyone was rich. However, their way and behavior were quite disturbing strange and weird. For everything by them was conducted according to wealth. The value of each and everyone's status was according to his

Sippurei Maasiyot – Chapter 12

wealth. That whoever has such and such thousands or tens-of-thousands has one status, and whoever has such and such, an amount of money has another status. And so forth the entire structure of societal value by them was aligned with the money each person had. And whoever has such and such thousands and tens-of-thousands in keeping with the sum which had been determined by them - he is king. And similarly, they had flags, that whoever has this much money is with this flag and has this particular status of that flag; and whoever has this much money is with another flag and has there the certain status of that flag, according to the value of his money. It had been determined by them how much money one should have to be considered of this flag with this particular status, and how much money another should have to be considered with another flag and its certain status. And so, the level and status of each and everyone was completely according to the money, as had been determined by them. Furthermore, it was fixed by them, if he has only this much money, he is a plain human, whereas if he has even less than this, he is an animal or bird, etc. So, by them they had wild animals and fowl, that is, if he has just this little money, he is called a human lion; and in a similar vein other wild animals and birds, etc., that in line with the small amount of money, he is just an animal or bird, etc. For the main thing by them was money, and the status and level of everyone was only according to the money.

Sippurei Maasiyot – Chapter 12

Now, it was heard in the world that there is such a country, and the **Ba'al Tefilah** would sigh deeply over this and would say, "Who knows how far they can go and err through this?" Some men from the Prayer Meister's retinue were present, and did not ask his opinion at all, but went there to that country to restore them to the good. For they the **Ba'al Tefilah's** associates had great pity on them about having gone so off in the lust for money; especially since the **Ba'al Tefilah** had said that they could go further and further astray, therefore these people went to that country. Perhaps they could restore them from their nonsense. So, the **Ba'al Tefilah's** people entered the country and approached one of them who was apparently a low status person whom they called an animal. And they began to talk with him, that truthfully money is not a purpose at all, and the main purpose is only serving Hashem Blessed his name, and so forth. But he did not listen to them at all, because it was already rooted in their thinking that the main thing is only money. And so did they chat with another, and he too did not listen. And they wanted to talk with him more, but he replied, "I have no more time to talk with you." They asked him, "Why?" He replied, "Because we all must leave the country and go to another country, for we have seen that the main goal is only money, therefore it has become ingrained in us that we must go to such a country where they make money. That is,

Sippurei Maasiyot – Chapter 12

there, there is a kind of earth from which they make gold and silver. Therefore, we all must now go to that country".

It also got into them that they wanted to have stars and constellations too, that is, whoever has so much and so much money, according to the amount they had determined for it, he should be a star, because since he has so much money he must have the power of the star, because the star generates the gold, because the fact that there is earth from which they make gold is, after all, due to the star that generates such earth there from which they make gold. Since the man has so much gold, he must have the power of the stars, therefore he himself is a star. And likewise, they said they wanted to have constellations too. That is, when someone would have so much and so much money, however much they had determined for it, he should be a constellation. And likewise, they made for themselves angels, all according to money. Until they agreed that they should have gods too, that whoever would have very much money, so many and so many thousands and myriads, however much they had determined for this, he would be a god, because since God gives him so much money, he himself is a god. They said furthermore that they ought not dwell in the air of this world, and they must not at all be together with other people, so that they should not contaminate them, because the other people of the world are completely impure compared to them; therefore, they decided that

Sippurei Maasiyot – Chapter 12

they should find for themselves very high mountains that are higher than all the world, and they should dwell there, so that they can be higher than the air of the world. They sent people to seek high mountains, and they found very high mountains. The whole country went and settled there on the high mountains; that is, on each mountain a gathering of people from the country in other words, a city settled, and around the mountain they made a big fortification and great trenches around the mountain, until it was impossible for any man to reach them, because there was no longer even a hidden path to the mountain, so that no other person would at all be able to reach them; and likewise on the next mountain, and so on all the mountains they always made a fortification etc. as mentioned. And they appointed guards far from the mountain, so no one would be able to reach them.

So, they dwelled there on the mountains and conducted themselves as mentioned earlier, and they had many gods, that is, according to money, as mentioned. However, since wealth was the main thing for them so much so that via great wealth a person could become a god - they had a fear of murder and theft, because anyone would be a murderer or thief in order to become a god via the money he would steal. But they said since the wealthy one is a god he will protect himself from theft and murder. And they established devotions and offerings to offer and pray to the gods, to get money

Sippurei Maasiyot – Chapter 12

through them, and they would sacrifice people and their very selves to the gods in order to be included in them and later be reincarnated as a rich [person]. Because their **Emunah** [main creed] was in money. And they had devotions, sacrifices and incenses with which they served their gods that is, those who had much money. But despite this the country was definitely full of murder and theft, because whoever did not believe in the devotions became a murderer and thief in order to get money, because the main thing for them was wealth, since through money one can buy anything - food and clothing - so the root of a man's life is through money; therefore, money was their main creed such was their foolish and confused thinking. And they all endeavored to not lose any money, because money was for them the fundamental creed and the god; on the contrary, they needed to try to bring money into the country from other places. Traders would go out from them to trade in other countries, in order to win money, in order to bring even more money into the country. And charity was certainly a great prohibition for them, because how can someone be permitted to give away the money that God has given him - which was for them the main thing, to have money - how can someone be permitted to give that away? So, for them it was definitely forbidden to give charity. And they had officers who were appointed to observe of everyone whether he has as much money as he says, because

Sippurei Maasiyot – Chapter 12

everyone had to show off his wealth at every moment in order to remain in the status and honor that he had according to his money in other words all the rich people who for them were gods, stars, angels etc. due to their money would always be inspected whether he has so much money; whether he is not in vain a god and so forth, and people were appointed to constantly watch this. And sometimes among them an animal would become a person, or a person an animal. Namely when a rich person lost his money, he already became a non-human - a man became an animal, because he already had no money for himself; and conversely when someone won money, so an animal became a human; and so on with the other classes, which by them was all according to money it was that way too, as sometimes one became a non-god because he has already lost the money. And they would have the figures and portraits of the gods that is, those who had much money, and everyone had the portraits, and they would hug and kiss them, because money was their entire devotion and religion.

And the Prayer Leader's people who were previously there in that country, returned to their place and they told the Prayer Leader of the nonsense of the country, how they were so fooled and lost in the craving of money, and that they wanted to already leave their country for another country where they make money as mentioned and wanted to make stars and constellations already. The Prayer Leader

Sippurei Maasiyot – Chapter 12

spoke up and said that he feared lest they stray more and more. Then people heard that they had already made themselves gods as mentioned. The Prayer Leader spoke up and said, "That is what I meant; that is why I feared" that is, by his always saying he feared lest they get further lost, he meant this. The Prayer Leader had great pity on them and came to the decision to personally go there; perhaps he would return them from their error. The Prayer Leader went there and came to the guards who stand around each mountain as mentioned. And the guards, it would reason, were people of low status who were able to stand in the air of this world, because the people who had status from their money were not at all able to be together with the people of the world and could not stand in the world's air, so that they should not contaminate them, and they were not at all able to speak with people of the world, so that they should not contaminate them with their breath in other words the foolish country considered the world entirely impure compared to them, as mentioned. Therefore, the guards who stood outside the city were surely of low status, except the guards also had the portraits of their gods and would hug and kiss them all the time, because with them too was money the main object of faith.

The Prayer Leader came to one of the guards and began talking with him about the ultimate purpose, inasmuch as the only ultimate purpose

Sippurei Maasiyot – Chapter 12

is Godly devotions - Torah, prayer, good deeds etc. and money is utter foolishness and not the ultimate purpose at all, etc. But the guard did not listen to him at all, for it was already ingrained in them for a long time that the main thing is only money, as mentioned. And likewise, the Prayer Leader went to all the guards and talked with them likewise as mentioned and they did not listen to him whatsoever. The Prayer Leader came to a decision and went into the city which was on the mountain as mentioned. When he arrived inside the city it was a great novelty to them and they asked, "How did you get in here?" since no one was able to reach them. He answered them, "Why do you ask? I am already inside the city, all the same." The Prayer Leader began talking with one of them about the purpose of the world, that money is no purpose at all, etc. as was his custom but the man did not listen to him at all, and likewise another, and likewise all of them, because they were already so lost in their mistake that they already could not listen to anybody, as mentioned. And it was a wonder to the people of the city that such a man exists and should come to them and say to them such things, the complete opposite of their faith. It struck them that this man must be the Prayer Leader, because they had already heard that there is such a Prayer Leader in the world, since the matter of the Prayer Leader had already become publicized in the world as mentioned,

Sippurei Maasiyot – Chapter 12

and people in the world would call him **Der Frummer Baal Tefilah** [the devout Prayer Leader]. But catch him they could not, because he would make himself appear different to each person: to one he appeared as a merchant, to another as a pauper, etc., immediately afterwards disappearing from there, in other words, he was quickly gone away.

And the day came to pass: now there was a **Gibbor** [Mighty Warrior], unto whom other **Gibborim** [warriors] had gathered. Now, the Warrior and his warriors were going around taking over countries, the Warrior wanting nothing else but submission in other words, that they should be subject under him. And when the people of the country submitted to him, he would release them; and if not - he would ruin them. So, he went around subjugating countries, without any desire for money whatsoever - only submission; that they should be under him. And the way of the Warrior was: he would send his warriors to a country when he was still very far from it - fifty miles - for them to surrender to him; and so, he was continually taking over countries.

And the merchants of the aforementioned wealthy country, who used to conduct trade in foreign countries, returned to their country and talked about the Warrior, and a great terror fell on them. And even though they were willing to submit themselves under him, the thing that prevented them was they heard that he loathes money and does not want any money at all, and this was contrary to their faith, therefore they could not submit themselves under him, because for them it would be like apostasy, since he did not at all believe in their creed, that is, in money. And they were very afraid of him, and they began to perform their devotions and bring their sacrifices to their gods that is, to those who had much money; and they would take a beastie that is, someone with little money, who was considered by them a beast and bring him for a sacrifice to their gods as mentioned, and similarly they performed their other devotions that is, the things with which they would serve their gods. And the Warrior was continually coming closer to them, and had started to send his warriors ahead to ask: What do they want? - after his usual custom, as mentioned. A great terror came over them and they did not know what to do.

Their own merchants gave them a suggestion: Inasmuch as they had been in a country where the entire populace were gods and traveled about with angels - that is, that country is where everyone, from the smallest to greatest, are all extraordinarily great **Vild-Groiss** [wild-great] wealthy people in the extreme, such that even the smallest among them is also a god according to their foolish delusion because the smallest person in the country is exceptionally wealthy and has as much money as was reckoned by them that with that much money one becomes a god, as mentioned. And they "travel with angels" since their horses are

Sippurei Maasiyot – Chapter 12

covered with such great wealth, with gold and so forth, that the covering of one horse was worth the amount that an angel had. Thus, the riders "travel with angels," tying three pairs of "angels" to a carriage and riding with them. "Therefore, you need to send to this country and they will surely help you, for they are all gods." All this was still the advice of their merchants. Their advice pleased them very much, for they believed that they would surely be saved by the other country, since they are all gods there, as mentioned.

And the Prayer Leader came to the decision he would go once again to that country; perhaps he would still lead them out of their folly. And he went there, came up to the guards, and began speaking with one guard in his usual way. The guard told him about the Warrior, that they are in great terror of him. The Prayer Leader asked him, "What do you have in mind to do?" The guard told him the matter mentioned above, that they want to send to the country where they are all gods etc. The Prayer Leader made much laughter of him and said to him, "That is quite a great folly! Because they are humans like we are. And all of you, with all your gods, are all merely humans and not one of them is any god at all. There is no more than only one God in the world: He who created everything, and He alone should be served and only to Him one should pray; and this alone is the main purpose in the world." And such other words did the Prayer Leader speak with the guard. And the

Sippurei Maasiyot – Chapter 12

Prayer Leader kept speaking more of the same kinds of words with the guard, while the guard continued to not listen, because their mistaken belief had already been set within them from a long time ago, as mentioned.

However, the Prayer Leader debated with him extensively, until finally the guard answered him, "What else can I do? I am only one individual, after all and compared to me are the numerous residents of the country." Now this already had the semblance of some **Teshuvah** [repentance], as the words which the Prayer Leader had spoken before with the guard, and the words which he spoke now, joined together until they stirred him somewhat. Because the **Teshuvah** that the guard had answered, "What can I do?" etc., made it known that the words of the Prayer Leader were starting to already enter his heart a little bit. And so, the Prayer Leader went to another guard and also spoke with him in his usual way, as above; and he too did not listen to him, but in the end also replied as above, "I am one person" and so forth, as above. And so, all the guards answered him this **Teshuvah** in the end.

Afterwards the Prayer Leader entered the city and began talking with them in his usual way: inasmuch as they are all very much in complete error, and money is no goal at all; rather, the essential purpose is solely to delve in Torah and prayer and so forth. They did not listen to him, for they were all very much rooted in money from a long time ago. And they told him

Sippurei Maasiyot – Chapter 12

about the Warrior, and that they want to send to the country where they are all gods, etc. He laughed at them too and told them that was a folly and they all are only humans, etc. "And they will be unable to help you at all, because you are human and they are human, and they are no god whatsoever. There is only one God, the All-Blessed One, etc." As for the Warrior he replied to them with a wondering expression, "Isn't this that Warrior?" the one he knows? They did not understand what he meant. And so, he went from one to the other, and continued talking thus with them, as above. And as for the Warrior he said to everyone, "Isn't this that Warrior?" etc., as above. They did not understand his words; what he meant. Meanwhile, a commotion broke out in the city, inasmuch as there was found someone who says such things, making laughter of their faith, and saying that there is only a single Unity, that is, Hashem Blessed his name, the All-Blessed One, etc.; and as for the Warrior, always saying, "Isn't this that Warrior?" etc. as above. They understood that this must certainly be the Prayer Leader, because he was already notorious among them, as mentioned. They ordered for him to be sought and caught. Even though he appeared different each time that is, at times presenting himself as a merchant, at times as a poor person, and so forth, wherefore they were not able to catch him, as mentioned, nonetheless they knew of this too, that the Prayer Leader constantly presents himself

Sippurei Maasiyot – Chapter 12

differently. They ordered an investigation into him, for him to be captured. He was sought out until they caught him, and they brought him to their elders.

When they began talking with him, he told them also as above, "You are all mistaken and in great folly, and this is no purpose whatsoever that is, money is no goal at all. Instead, there exists a singular all-blessed One, namely the Creator, blessed be His name, who has created everything. He alone should be served, and money is an utter nonsense, etc. And the country where you say they are all gods - they will be unable to help you whatsoever, for they are only human, etc." They considered him insane, because the entire country was already so immersed in money and they were already so crazed that whoever said something contrary to their foolishness was for them a madman.

They asked him, "What is this that you say about the Warrior, Isn't this that Warrior?" as above. He answered them, "Inasmuch as I used to be with a King, and to the King a Warrior was lost; then if this is that Warrior, I am acquainted with him. And furthermore, you're relying on the country where you say they are all gods - this is nonsense, because they will be unable to help you whatsoever. Just the reverse - this will be your very downfall, if you rely on them." They asked him, "Where do you know this from?" He answered them: Insofar as the King whom he was with, had with him a **YAD** [Hand] That is, the King had something

Sippurei Maasiyot – Chapter 12

resembling a hand with five fingers and with all the grooves that is, all the creases and ruts that are on a hand. And the Hand was the map of all the worlds, and all that has been since the creation of heaven and earth until the end and what will be afterwards was all depicted on the Hand. For depicted in the scratches and folds of the Hand was the diagram of all the worlds, how every world stands, with all of every world's thing in detail, everything standing out on the and as depicted on a land map as is known to those who are used to land maps, that is, depicted on a paper is each town, every country and every bridge; and similarly other things: streams, woods etc.; and by everything it is all written down, that this is this town and this is that country and so forth.

Thus, all the worlds were depicted on the Hand by the ruts and folds of the Hand, and in the Hand's, ruts were as if letters, just as letters are inscribed on a map next to each thing so that they may know what it is, that is, that they should know that here is this town and here is this stream and likewise other things. In exactly the same way by the ruts of the Hand were depicted the likeness of letters next to everything depicted on the Hand so as to know what is everything depicted there. The same for every separate city, every town and all the rivers, bridges, mountains and other objects whatever is found in the world and in all the worlds: everything was depicted on the Hand by the ruts and folds on the Hand, and there were always letters standing next to everything, that this is this thing and that is that thing, etc. Similarly, all the people who go around in every country, and all their experiences that is, everything that passes over a man during his lifetime, were all depicted on the Hand. "And even all the paths from one country to another, and from one place to another, were written on it, and on account of that I knew the way to come in here to this town which no man can enter because the wealthy country had dug around their cities and nobody could come to them, as above. And so, if you want to send me into the other town, I know that way too, all through the Hand. And also imprinted on the Hand was the way from one world to another world. For there is a path and a course on which one can ascend from earth to heaven for, one cannot go up from earth to heaven, due to not knowing the way; but depicted there was the way to go up to heaven. So depicted there were all the paths that exist from one world to another world. For, Eliyahu ascended to heaven with this path, and that path was written there; **Moshe Rabbeinu** went up to heaven with a different path, and that other path was also written there; and likewise, **Chanokh** [Enoch] ascended to heaven with yet another path, and that path was also written there. Thus, from one world to the other farther, higher world was all depicted by the ruts and folds of the Hand.

Sippurei Maasiyot – Chapter 12

Also represented on the Hand was everything as it was at the time the world was created, as it is now, and as it will be afterwards. For instance, the city of **Sedom** [Sodom] was depicted there as that city had been while inhabited before it was overturned; in addition, depicted there was **Sedom** being upheaved, as a city turning over; and again, depicted there was **Sedom** as it appears today after the upheaval. For on the Hand was depicted what was, what is, and what will be. And there on the Hand I have seen that the country of which you say they are all gods, together with all the people who come to them for help that is, that the city should help them will both all be obliterated." All this the Prayer Leader told them.

This was an extraordinary novelty to them, for it was recognized that this is true talk, because it is known that on a map all things are depicted, so they understood that his words are true since such things cannot be thought up, because one can see for himself that he can put together two ruts of the hand and a letter will become of them. For this reason, they understood this is no contrived thing; hence it was an extraordinary novelty to them. They asked him, "Whereabout is the King? Perhaps he will show us a way how to find money".

He answered them, with an expression of someone awestruck and angered, "You still want money?! Don't talk about money at all!" They asked him, "Nonetheless, tell us where

Sippurei Maasiyot – Chapter 12

the King is." He answered them, "I too don't know of the King; where he is. And this is how the story happened: "Once, there was a King and a Queen, and they had an only daughter. And it came near the time to marry her off, so they seated advisors to give counsel as to whom she ought to be married off to. And I too that is, the Prayer Leader, who is still relating this in front of them was there among the advisors, because the King liked me, and my advice was that they should give her the Warrior, because the Warrior had wrought us many benefits, for he had conquered many countries; therefore, he ought to be given the Queen's Daughter for a wife. My advice was very liked and they all agreed upon it, and there was a big celebration there for having found a groom for the Queen's Daughter. And they wed the Queen's Daughter with the Warrior, and the Queen's Daughter had a Child. And the Baby was quite an extraordinary beauty, being no sort of human beauty whatsoever: his hair was golden and had all the colors, his face was like the sun and his eyes were other luminaries. And the Child was born with mature wisdom, because they saw in him immediately when he was born that he is already a great sage, for when people were talking, in the place where one needs to laugh, he would laugh; and so, with other such things they likewise recognized him being a great sage - except not yet having the motions of an adult, namely he had not yet the faculty of speech and other such things - but

Sippurei Maasiyot – Chapter 12

this they saw right away: that he is already a big genius.

And with the King was an Orator, that is, a speaker who is a master of language and rhetoric, who was able to talk very fine talk: very beautiful speeches, songs and praises for the King. And the Orator was on his own account a fine Orator too, but the King showed him the hidden path and the way for him to go up and get the power of the science of rhetoric, and thereby he became a very superb orator. The King also had a Sage, and the Sage was also a sage on his own account, but the King showed him the way for him to go up and get wisdom, and thereby he became an extraordinary, superb sage. And similarly, the Warrior was mighty on his own, but the King showed him the way for him to go and get strength, and thereby he became an extraordinary, superb warrior. For, there is a Sword that hangs in the air, and the Sword has three powers. When the Sword is lifted then all the officers of the opposing army flee, so as a matter of course they fall, because when the officers flee, there is no one to lead the battle, so they certainly fall. But despite this, the survivors may still be able to wage war - however, the Sword has two sharp edges, and they have two powers: through one edge they all fall down, and through the other edge they get the sickness called **dör** [wasting] namely they the enemies whom they are fighting become meager of flesh and lifeless, as is

Sippurei Maasiyot – Chapter 12

known of this sickness; the Merciful One spare us. So, by merely making a move with the Sword in its place, the enemies are stricken with the aforementioned things, that is, by using one edge the enemies have defeat, and by using the other edge the enemies are stricken with **dör**, as mentioned. And the King showed the Warrior the path that there is to the Sword and from there he attained his great strength.

And to me the King also showed the way to get my thing; I got from there what I need. In other words, the Prayer Leader, who is telling all this, said that the King showed him the way from which he should get his thing, namely, prayer.

And likewise, the King had a **Ohev Ne'eman** [Faithful Friend] who was in love with the King with a very extraordinary love. They loved each other so much that it was utterly impossible for them to be one without seeing the other for some amount of time. But nonetheless there must be times when they need to be apart, so they had portraits in which both their images were depicted. They would delight themselves in other words, take pleasure and satisfaction with the portraits when they could not see each other. And the images depicted how the King and his Faithful Friend love each other and hug and kiss each other with great love. And the portraits had the special ability that whoever looked at the images attained great love in other words, one received the trait of love when looking at the images. And the Faithful Friend also received

Sippurei Maasiyot – Chapter 12

the love that is, the amorousness from the place which the King showed him.

There came the time when they all went, each one to his place, to receive there his power for his thing - that is, the Orator, the Warrior, and all the King's people, each went up to his place to renew his power. And the day came to pass: there was a very great Storm Wind upon the world. And the Storm Wind mixed up the entire world, and overturned sea to dry land and dry land to sea, and wilderness to settled area and settled area to wilderness; so, it overturned the entire world. And the Storm Wind went into the King's chamber and did nothing at all there in other words, there at the King's it wrought absolutely no damage, except that the Storm Wind went in and snatched away the aforementioned Child of the Queen's Daughter. And amidst the commotion, as soon as the Storm Wind snatched away the dear Child, the Queen's Daughter followed [him] immediately in other words, the Princess immediately started running after the Child in order to snatch him back; she too went off someplace no one knows where. So too the Queen, and so too the King: they all went after the Child, until they all became dispersed and no one knows where they are. But all of us were nowhere nearby during this, for we were gone away then, each to his place to renew his power, as mentioned; and when we came back, we could no longer find them all, as mentioned. The Hand too became missing then.

Sippurei Maasiyot – Chapter 12

So, from that time on we have all become scattered and can no longer each go to his place to renew his power, for since the entire world has been overturned, we now need different paths today; therefore, we have no longer gone up each to his place to renew his power. However, the impression that remains by each of us meaning the token, that is, the little bit that has remained by each one from long ago is also very great - and if this mighty one which the country feared is the King's Warrior, he is certainly a very mighty warrior. [All this the Prayer Leader told the people.]

And they heard out his words and were very amazed, and now they held the Prayer Leader fast by him and would no longer let him go from them because perhaps the warrior upon them is the King's Warrior mentioned above, with whom the Prayer Leader is acquainted. And the aforementioned Warrior kept coming closer to the country, always sending his emissaries to them, until he reached the country. And he stationed himself below the city and sent his emissaries inside to them for them to tell him what they want: to submit themselves or not, as above. They were very terrified of him and they begged the Prayer Leader that he should give them a suggestion. The Prayer leader told them it was necessary to inspect the conduct of this warrior in order for him to recognize thereby if this is the aforementioned Warrior of the King. The Prayer Leader left and went out towards the

Sippurei Maasiyot – Chapter 12

Warrior, and he reached the Warrior's army and began talking with one from among the Warrior's accompanying warriors that is, with one of his sentries in order to examine if he is the Warrior with whom he is familiar. The Prayer Leader asked him, "What are your doings? And how have you gotten together with the Warrior?" He answered him that is, that same warrior replied to the Prayer Leader, "What took place was like this: It is written in their chronicles how there had been a great Storm Wind upon the world, changing sea to dry land and dry land to sea, and wilderness to settled area and settled area to wilderness, mixing up the entire world. And after the noise and upheaval, the entire world having become so mixed up, the world's people decided to make a king for themselves. They started to investigate who ought to be made king over them and they reasoned, 'Inasmuch as the essential thing is only the ultimate **Takhlith** [purpose] therefore whoever most occupies himself with and exerts himself in the purpose of the world - he deserves to be king. They began probing what is the purpose, and there arose several opinions among them.

One faction said that the main object is an honor, for, 'We see that the world considers honoring the main thing. Because when a person is not given his respect - that is, when some word is uttered against his honor - he experiences bloodshed, because the main thing is an honor, for the entire world. And even after death, people are careful to give to the dead his honor, burying him with respect and so forth and telling him, 'What is being done for you is all being done on account of your honor. Even though after death one no longer wants any money and the dead person certainly has no desire for anything, nevertheless they are particular about the dead's honor and they guard his honor. Therefore, it is an honor that is the main object. They continued saying more such conjectures and deductions of that sort, that honor is the main object of the world, until it became settled among them that the main purpose is an honor. Therefore, they needed to search for an honorable person, that is to say, a person who attains honor and moreover, the person should also pursue honor, for since he receives honor and pursues it, and assists human nature which desires honor, therefore this person exerts himself and pursues after the main goal and has reached it, because the goal is, after all, honor, as mentioned; therefore, such a person deserves to be king." All this was the foolish opinion of one sect of them, and so they found foolish conjectures and deductions until they became led astray therein and said that honor is the purpose. Likewise, all the other factions that will appear below all had foolish reasonings for their foolish notions, this is why the man deserves to be king.

They went searching for such a person and they went and saw an old Gypsy beggar being carried while following him were perhaps five

Sippurei Maasiyot – Chapter 12

hundred Gypsies. And the beggar was blind, hunchback and mute, and all these people followed him because they all were his relatives, for he had sisters, brothers, and the seed of his loins, until there came to be so many of them, all of whom followed him and carried him. And the old beggar was very particular about his honor, for he was a very angry person and always heaped his great indignation upon them, always ordering that other should carry him and always scolding them. Hence this elderly beggar is a very **Honorable** man because he has such an honor, and also pursues honor, because he is so strict over his honor. Therefore, this beggar pleased them and they accepted him as a king. And because land also has an effect, for there is a land that engenders and is conducive to honor, and similarly there is a land that is especially suited for another trait, therefore this faction which regarded honor as the main purpose sought a country that engenders and is conducive to honor; and they found such a country that is conducive to it and they settled there.

One faction said that the main object is not honor, and they conceived that the main object is murder, for, we see that all the things that are found on the earth - grasses and all plants and people, and all that is in the entire world - must all ultimately cease to exist. Hence the very goal of all things is to be finished off the hat is destroyed. Therefore, a murderer who kills and destroys people is really bringing the world to

Sippurei Maasiyot – Chapter 12

its purpose. Therefore, they came to the conclusion that the goal is murder. They looked for a person who would be a murderer; an angry person and an extremely vengeful person, for such a person, is closest to the purpose, according to their deluded mindset and he deserves to be king. They went looking for such a person and they heard a shriek. They asked - What is this, such a screech?! "They replied to them this shriek is: someone has slaughtered his father and mother. They spoke up, where else can one find such a stronghearted and angry murderer, that he should murder his own father and mother? This here man has reached the purpose that is, the one who has slaughtered father and mother! And they were extremely pleased by him and they accepted him as a king over them. And they sought for themselves a country that causes that is, brings about murder and they chose a place among mountains where killers abide and they went there and settled there with their king.

A faction said that he deserves to be a king who has a great abundance of food and does not eat the fare of other people but only fine foods such as milk so that his mind should not become coarse; such a person ought to be king. However, they could not immediately find such a person who would not eat the foods of other people. In the meantime, they chose for themselves a rich man who had plenty of food and whose food was a bit finer until they would

Sippurei Maasiyot – Chapter 12

find such a person as they want, who would not eat, etc. as above. And meanwhile, they made the rich man into a king until they would find such a person as they want, as above; then the rich man would descend from the reign and the other one would be taken up as a king. And they chose for themselves a country suited for this and they went and settled there.

A faction said that a beautiful woman is fit to be king, for the main object is, after all, that the world should be inhabited with people since for that reason the world was created. And since a beautiful woman brings about that desire, through which the habitation of the world grows greater since more people come about, it follows she brings the world to the goal. Therefore, a beautiful woman deserves to be king. They chose for themselves a beautiful woman and she became king over them. And they sought for themselves a land conducive to this, and they went there and settled there.

A faction said that the main object is speech, because the distinction between a man and a beast is only speech, and since that is essential in which a man is greater than a beast, therefore it is the main purpose that is speech. They sought for themselves a speaker that is, a talker who would be eloquent and who would know many languages and would always talk a great deal all the time, for such a person is at the goal. They went and found a French lunatic who was going around and talking to himself. They asked him if he knows languages, and he knew

Sippurei Maasiyot – Chapter 12

several languages. Now such a man has certainly already reached the goal according to their foolish deluded ideas, since he is a master of language, knows many languages, and talks a great deal - for the talks even to himself, after all! Therefore, they were very pleased by him and they accepted him as a king. And they chose for themselves a land conducive to this and they went and settled there with their king. And he surely led them on the straight path!

A faction said that the main purpose is happiness. For, when a boy is born, people are happy; when there is a wedding, people are happy; when conquering a country, people are happy. It follows that the main purpose of everything is only happiness. Therefore, they sought a man who would always be happy, for he is, after all, at the goal, and he should be king over them. They went searching and they saw a gentile going along with a disgusting shirt and carrying a bottle of brandy while following him were several other gentiles. And this gentile was very happy because he was very drunk. They saw that this gentile is very happy and has no concern whatsoever, and they liked him very much, this gentile because he has reached the goal since the goal is only happiness. They accepted him as a king over them, and surely, he led them on the right path! And they chose for themselves a land conducive to this, that is, where there are vineyards so that they should make wine, and from the seeds of the grapes they would make

Sippurei Maasiyot – Chapter 12

Brandywine; and nothing whatsoever of the grape bunches should go to waste, because this for them was the main purpose: to drink and got drunk and always be happy, even though one doesn't know at all about what, for they had nothing at all to be happy about. Nevertheless, it was the main purpose for them to be always happy. And they chose for themselves a land conducive to this, as above, and they went and settled there.

A faction said that the main thing is wisdom. They sought for themselves a great sage and made him a king over them, and they sought for themselves a land conducive to wisdom and they went and settled there.

A faction said that the main goal is to attend to oneself with food and drink, which is called **Pilevin**, in order to enlarge his **Evarim** [limbs]. And they sought a **Ba`al Evarim** [master of limbs], that is, someone who has large limbs and nurses himself to grow his limbs that is, the members of the body, for since he has big limbs he has, after all, a larger portion in the world because he takes up more space in the world. So, this man is closer to the purpose because the purpose is, after all, to grow the limbs; therefore, such a person ought to be a king. They went and found a tall man which is called a **Veynger** [Hand]; they were pleased by him because he has, after all, large limbs and is at the goal. They accepted him as a king and they sought a land conducive to this and they went and settled there.

Sippurei Maasiyot – Chapter 12

And there was a different group that said that all these things are no goal at all; instead, the right purpose is to only be involved in prayer to Hashem Blessed his name, and to be a humble person and a lowly person, etc. In other words, one should not deem anything of oneself, etc. And they sought for themselves a prayer leader, and they made him a king over them." One will understand by himself already that all the previous factions were all gravely mistaken and deluded in great folly, each faction in their folly through their foolish hypotheses and foolish deductions. Only this last faction hit the truth proper - so, fortunate are they!

All this was related by one of the strongmen before the Prayer Leader. And he went on to tell him that they namely the strongmen who joined themselves to the Warrior as mentioned - they are from the faction of the limb-masters mentioned above that is, the faction that said that the main object is only to nurse oneself to grow his limbs who had taken up as a king over themselves a master of limbs that is, a large person, as mentioned. "And the day came to pass, and a **Machneh** [Company] of them were going along in other words, a great deal of the **Ample-Aimbed** people were going along, with wagons in **Ibez** [train] bringing along food, drink, and other such things. Now, of these large-limbed ones the world was certainly very afraid, for they were large and mighty men, and whoever encountered them was sure to step off the road. Meanwhile, as the camp of the ample-

Sippurei Maasiyot – Chapter 12

limbed was going along like that, up against them from the opposite direction came a big **Warrior** [mighty one] and this was the Warrior who now goes with them. And this Warrior did not step off the road for them and he went into the camp and dispersed them here and there, and the people of the camp were terrified of him. And he that is, the Warrior went inside among the aforementioned wagons which trailed behind them and ate up everything that was there. This was an extraordinary novelty to them that he is such a mighty man that he is not afraid of them whatsoever and entered among them and ate up all that was on the wagons so they immediately fell down before him, saying immediately, **Hail** [live] the king meaning they immediately made him a king! because he certainly deserves the reign, according to their notion that the main accomplishment is someone who is ample-limbed, as mentioned. And their king will certainly forgo the kingship for him because since he is so strong and so well-limbed that he certainly deserves the reign. And so it was: they took him up as king that is, the Warrior who came against them, as mentioned. And this is the Warrior with whom we now go about conquering the world. But he says that is, the Warrior who has now become king over them that he means something else in his going about conquering the world, for he does not at all intend that the world should be under him; instead, he means something else." All this, one of the strongmen told the Prayer

Sippurei Maasiyot – Chapter 12

Leader who had asked him how they had joined the Warrior; he answered him all this.

Asked the Prayer Leader, "Wherein is the strength of the Warrior who is now your king?" He answered him, "Inasmuch as there was a country that did not want to submit themselves under him, the Warrior took his Sword which he has, and his Sword has three powers: when it is lifted, all the army officers flee" etc. and he recounted the three powers explained above, from which the King's Warrior got his strength, as mentioned.

When the Prayer Leader heard this, he realized that this is definitely the King's Warrior mentioned above. The Prayer Leader asked if it were possible to be seen by the Warrior who is their king. They answered him it must be announced for approval before him. They went and announced, and he summoned that he should come in, and the Prayer Leader entered to the Warrior. When the Prayer Leader entered the Warrior, they recognized each other and there was very great rejoicing between them over their being privileged to reunite together. And between them was rejoicing and crying happiness and weeping, for they recalled the King and his men - they cried over that - therefore between them was rejoicing and crying. The Prayer Leader began to discuss with the Warrior what experiences they had arrived here.

The Warrior told the Prayer Leader that from the time that there was the Storm Wind - when

Sippurei Maasiyot – Chapter 12

they all became dispersed - when he returned from where he went to renew his power and did not find the King with all his people, as mentioned, he then let himself go wherever he would go. And he passed by them all: that is, he understood he was at the place where the King is and where all his people are. That is, he was at a certain place and he understood that there is certainly where the King is found, however, he was unable to seek and find him. And similarly, he passed by another place, understanding that the Queen is certainly there, however he was unable to seek and find her, and thus he passed by all the King's people.

Only you have I not passed by!" That is, the Warrior who is telling this said to the Prayer Leader that he passed by all the places of all the people; only the place of the Prayer Leader did he not pass by. The Prayer Leader replied to him saying, "I passed by all their places, and by your place as well. For, I was passing by a certain place and I saw the King's crown standing there and I understood that the King is certainly here, however I was unable to seek and find him. And so, I went further and passed by a sea of blood and I understood that this sea is certainly made from the tears of the Queen who weeps over all this and the Queen is certainly here, however I could not seek and find her. And so, I passed by a sea of milk and I understood that the sea is certainly made from the milk of the Queen's Daughter whose son was lost, and the milk pressured her and from

Sippurei Maasiyot – Chapter 12

this the sea of milk came to be; and the Queen's Daughter is certainly here, however I was unable to seek and find her. And so, I went further and saw the golden hairs of the Child laid out, and I did not take from them whatsoever, and I knew that the Child is certainly here, however it was not possible to seek and find him. And so, I went further and was passing by a sea of wine and I knew that this sea is certainly made from the speech of the Orator, who stands and speaks consolations before the King and the Queen, and then turns his face and speaks consolations to the Queen's Daughter, and from his speech the sea of wine comes to be as written - And the roof of your mouth is like best wine. However, I could not find him. And so, I went further, and I saw a stone standing thereupon which was etched out just like the Hand' with its ruts that is, just like the Hand with all the furrows, etc. which had been at the King's, as mentioned, and I understood that the Sage of the King is certainly here and the Sage has engraved for himself the shape of the Hand on the stone, but it was not possible to find him. And so, I went further and I saw arranged on a mountain the golden tables, the **Credenzas** [display cupboards] and the rest of the King's treasures, and I understood that the King's Treasurer is certainly here, however it was impossible to find him." All this the Prayer Leader told over to the Warrior.

Replied the Warrior, "I too passed by all these

Sippurei Maasiyot – Chapter 12

places, and I did take from the golden hair of the child, for I took seven hairs that had all sorts of colors, and they are very dear to me. And I settled down and sustained myself with whatever possible, with grass and so forth, until I had nothing whatsoever to sustain myself. I let myself go where I would go, and when I went away from my place, I forgot my bow there." The Prayer Leader replied, "I saw your bow! And I knew that it was certainly your bow, but I could not find you." The Warrior went on telling the Prayer Leader that, "When I went away from the place, I went until I encountered the troops mentioned above that is, the troop of the ample-limbed mighty men mentioned above, and I entered in their midst because I was very hungry and wanted to eat; and as soon as I entered among them, they immediately took me up as a king, as mentioned. And now I go conquering the world, and my intention is: perhaps I will be able to find the King and his people mentioned above".

The Prayer Leader began discussing with the Warrior: "What to do with these people!?" That is, with the country that is so fallen into craving money until they have gone out to such extraordinary folly that those who have much money are gods for them; and so, forth the other follies the country has. The Warrior answered the Prayer Leader that he had heard from the King that one can take out from any craving someone who has fallen into it except

Sippurei Maasiyot – Chapter 12

someone who has fallen in the lust for money; it is impossible to extract him from it by any means. "Therefore, you will have no effect on them whatsoever, for it is impossible to extract them from this at all. Albeit through the way that there is to the Sword mentioned above" - from where he gets his power as mentioned - "only through this way can one extract from the lust of money someone who has sunk into it." So, he had heard from the King. The Warrior remained together with the Prayer Leader for a while, and as for the country which had beseeched the Prayer Leader that he should go out to the Warrior on their behalf, as mentioned, they extended the time. That is, the Prayer Leader convinced the Warrior that he should give them a span that is, until which he should do nothing at all to them. He allowed their time, then they made signs between themselves, that is, the Prayer Leader and the Warrior exchanged signs so that one would be able to get information from the other, then the Prayer Leader went off on his way.

As the Prayer Leader went on, he saw people going along and entreating God Blessed is He, praying and carrying prayer books. He was afraid of them and they were frightened of him too. He stood to pray, and they also stood to pray. Then he asked them, "Who are you?" They answered him, "Inasmuch as when there was the Storm Wind, the world separated into many factions, these choosing this thing, and those choosing that thing, just as all the

Sippurei Maasiyot – Chapter 12

different factions are explained above. At that time, we chose for ourselves that the main purpose is only to be constantly involved in prayer to Hashem Blessed his name. We sought and found a master of prayer and made him a king".

When the Prayer Leader heard this, it pleased him exceptionally, for this is what he himself wants. He began to talk with them and showed them the order of his prayers and his books and the ideas he had regarding prayers. When they heard his talk, their eyes opened and they saw the greatness of the Prayer Leader. They immediately made him a king over them, for their king deferred the kingship to him since they saw that he is quite a great man. that he is set apart on a very, very high level. The Prayer Leader taught them and opened their eyes and showed them how to pray to Hashem Blessed his name, and he made them into very great complete tzaddikim, for they had been tzaddikim before as well since they had involved themselves only in prayer, albeit the Prayer Leader opened their eyes until they became extremely great tzaddikim. The Prayer Leader sent a letter to the Warrior and informed him how he was privileged and had found such people as he wants and had become king over them.

Now the aforementioned country that is, the wealthy land for whom money was the main object, etc. as mentioned continued occupying themselves with their devotions that is, they

Sippurei Maasiyot – Chapter 12

kept doing wild things and offering sacrifices to their gods, that is, to those who had much money, as mentioned, and the time that the Warrior had granted them was already about to run out. They were very frightened and they did their devotions and offered sacrifices and incense and involved themselves in their prayers which they prayed to their gods. They caught a **Chayeleh** [little critter], that is, such a person who has little money, and offered him for a sacrifice to their gods. And it remained their opinion that they must perform their first plan which they had been given, that they should send to the country where they are all gods there because they have very extraordinary riches there which according to their opinion entails that they are all gods and that country would certainly save them, since they are all gods after all, as mentioned. They did so, and they sent emissaries there to that country.

Meanwhile on the way as the emissaries were going, they went astray and they noticed a man walking with a stick, whose stick came to more than all their gods. That is, his stick was set with very expensive diamonds so that the stick was worth more than the riches of all their gods. Should one put together all the riches of their gods and even of the gods of that country they're going to, the stick would be worth more than all their riches. Furthermore, the man was walking with a hat in which there were diamonds so that the hat was also worth

Sippurei Maasiyot – Chapter 12

extraordinarily much. As soon as the emissaries noticed this man they immediately fell down before him in kneeling and prostration that is, they bowed profusely before him, because according to their foolish opinion this man is a god over all gods, for he has such extraordinarily great riches. And this man whom they encountered was the King's Treasurer mentioned above.

The man said to them, "This here is a novelty for you!? Come with me - I'll show you riches!" He led them atop the mountain where the King's treasury was laid out in order and he showed them the treasure. As soon as they saw the treasure, they immediately fell down with bowing and prostration, because he is, after all, a god over all gods according to their foolish and deluded opinion, as for them the essence of the creed was money, as mentioned. Albeit they brought no sacrifices, for in accordance with their belief that he is such a god, etc. they certainly would have offered themselves to him, however when these emissaries went out the emissaries were warned that on the way they should offer no sacrifices, for they were afraid that should they want to offer sacrifices along the way, none of them would remain, for maybe one of them will find a treasure on the road. Maybe one of them will enter an outhouse and find a treasure. he will want to sacrifice himself to it, and none of them will remain; therefore, the country warned the emissaries that on the way they should offer no sacrifices

Sippurei Maasiyot – Chapter 12

whatsoever.

The emissaries came to the decision: Why should they any longer go to those other gods, that is, to the country they were sent to, where they are greatly wealthy people whom they considered to be gods? Isn't it better than this man will surely be able to better help them, for he is, after all, a god above all of them according to their crazed notion, since he has such extraordinary, great riches more than them all many, many times over? Therefore, they beseeched this man that he should go with them into their country. He was amenable with them and went with them and entered their country. There was a great celebration in the country, that they had acquired such a god, for they were already sure now that through him they would have a deliverance, for he is such a god, since he has, after all, such great fortune. The man who was the King's Treasurer, as mentioned, who was accepted by the countrymen as God ordered that until there would be a proper order in the country, no one in the meantime should offer any sacrifices. For this Warden was in fact a great tzaddik, for he was of the King's people, who were all very great tzaddikim. The Warden certainly loathed the foolish practices of the country but he was still incapable of leading them out of their evil way; however, for the time being, he ordered them that in any case no sacrifices should be brought. The countrymen started beseeching him regarding the aforementioned Warrior of whom they were very terrified, and the Warden also replied to them, "Could this be the Warrior whom he knows"?

The Warden got up and went out to the Warrior and asked the Warrior's people if it were possible to be seen by him, and they said they would announce it. They announced it. He ordered for him, to be let in, and the Warden entered before the Warrior. They recognized each other, and there was a celebration and crying between them, as above that is, they were very happy that they were privileged to find each other but they still wept very much: how can the rest of the aforementioned people be brought as well? The Warrior spoke up to the Warden, "Our kosher Prayer Leader is also here, and I have already seen him, and he has already become a king!" And they told each other how it had evolved that they arrived here. The Warden told the Warrior that he had passed by everyone, that is, by the King's place and all the aforementioned people; only by the two of them did he not pass, that is, by the place of the Prayer Leader and the Warrior he did not pass. The Warden talked with the Warrior about the country that has become so errant and so deluded in money that they have fallen into such nonsense.

The Warrior answered the Warden that which he had told the Prayer Leader, that he had heard from the King that whoever has fallen into the craving of money cannot be taken out of it by any means except by that way as mentioned.

Sippurei Maasiyot – Chapter 12

Again, they extended time: that is, the Warden convinced the Warrior that he should give the country yet another date. The Warrior gave them another date. Then they made signals between themselves - the Warden and the Warrior - and the Warden went away from the Warrior and returned to that country. Now, the Warden certainly kept rebuking them severely over their evil way in which they had become so abased in craving money, but he could not lead them out of it, since they were already very deep-rooted in it. Nevertheless, since the Prayer Leader and the Warden had talked with them very much, they had already become a little confused and kept saying, "**Aderaba** [Just the reverse]! Take us out of it!" Even though they still held themselves fast in their foolish notion and did not want to get out of their nonsense at all, nevertheless they kept saying when they were rebuked, "**Aderaba** - if it is indeed so that we are mistaken, **NA** [please] take us out of our error"!

The Warden replied to them, "I will give you a suggestion against the Warrior. I know the Warrior's power and from where he gets his strength." And he told them the matter of the Sword, mentioned above, from where the Warrior gets his strength. "Therefore, I will go with you to the place of the Sword, and by this, you will be able to stand up against the Warrior for you will also get strength from there." And the Warden's intention was: when they arrive at the Sword's place, they will already be out from

Sippurei Maasiyot – Chapter 12

their money craving for by means of that way to the Sword, thereby a person gets out of the money craving, as mentioned. The country accepted his advice and sent their magnates who to them were gods and they went together with the Warden to the Sword. And the gods, that is, their magnates who went with the Warden certainly went dressed in gold and silver jewelry since this was the main thing for them. So, they went together, the Warden and the country's magnates whom they called gods. **The** Warden made the thing known to the Warrior, inasmuch as he is going with them to seek the place of the Sword and his intention is maybe he will be privileged on the way to find the King and his people. The Warrior replied, "I too will go with you." The Warrior disguised himself so that the people going with the Warden should not know that he himself is the Warrior and also went with the Warden. They decided the Warden and the Warrior would inform the Prayer Leader of this as well. They informed him, and The Prayer Leader replied he will also go with them. The Prayer Leader went to them and the Prayer Leader ordered his people before he went away that they should pray about this, that Hashem Blessed his name, should make their venture successful; that they should be privileged to find the King and his people. For the Prayer Leader had always kept praying about this, that the King and his people should be found, and always kept ordering his people that they should also pray about this,

Sippurei Maasiyot – Chapter 12

and he had composed prayers for them which they should pray for this; and now that he wanted to go the Warden and the Warrior so that they should go together to search for the King and his people, he urged them, even more, to pray for it constantly that they should be privileged to find them. The Prayer Leader came to the Warden and the Warrior and there was certainly great rejoicing among them - celebration and weeping, as before. They, all three, went together, that is, the Warden, the Warrior, and the Prayer Leader, with the "gods," that is, the country's magnates who were called "gods" in their country going with them.

They went and went, and they came to a certain country, and there were guards there standing around the country. They asked the sentries, "What sort of country is this, and who is your king?" The guards replied: Inasmuch as when there was the Storm Wind, at which time the world became separated into numerous factions that is, into many opinions, as each sect had a different opinion, as mentioned, then the people of the country chose for themselves that the main thing is wisdom, and they took up for themselves a great sage as a king. Not long ago they found quite an exceptionally great wise man, who is strangely an extraordinarily great sage. The king relinquished the kingship to him and they took him up as king, since for them the main thing was wisdom. The three of them said that is, the Warden, the Warrior, and

Sippurei Maasiyot – Chapter 12

the Prayer Leader that it appears that this must be our Sage that is, the King's Sage. They asked if it were possible to be seen by him, and they answered them, "It must be announced." They went and announced, and he ordered them to come in. They that is, the three of them entered into the Sage, who had become king in the country. They recognized each other, for this sage was indeed the King's Sage mentioned earlier. There was certainly great celebration there - rejoicing and weeping, for they wept, "How to be privileged to find the King and the others as well"!?

They asked the Sage if he knows anything about the King's Hand. He answered them that the Hand is with him, but since the time that they had become dispersed by the Storm Wind - from that time onward he does not want to gaze at the Hand at all, because the Hand belongs exclusively to the King. Albeit, he had carved out the Hand's form on a stone in order to use it a little for his wisdom but upon the Hand itself, he doesn't look at all.

They discussed with the Sage how he had come here, and he told them that since the time the Storm Wind happened, he went where he would go and as he went, he passed by everyone. of the King's people; only by the three of them, that is, by the place of the Prayer Leader, the Warrior, and the Warden he did not pass by until this country found him and took him up as a king; and now in the meantime, he must guide them according to their way,

Sippurei Maasiyot – Chapter 12

according to their sophistries, until later he will lead them out to the truth proper.

They talked with the Sage regarding that country that had become so deluded about money, etc., and they said, "If we had been thrown around and dispersed for nothing more than on account of that country, in order that we should correct them and turn them to the truth, it would also be worth it, for they have become so deluded." Because in truth, all the aforementioned factions, each one having chosen its nonsense, this one wanting honor, and this one murder, etc. - they have all become deluded and need to be led out to the proper goal. For even the sect that had chosen for itself that the main thing is wisdom, they too have not reached the true purpose and also need to be led out from that, for they have clung to alien and heretical wisdom. Still, one can more easily lead people out of all the other follies, except these ones are so deluded in the idols of money and are so fallen into it that it is impossible to extract them from it. And the Sage also replied to them that he too had heard from the King that it is possible to extract someone who has fallen into any craving, but from the craving of money, it is impossible to extract, other than by the way that there is to the Sword, as mentioned. The Sage said he too would go with them, and they all four went along, and the **gods** that is, the wealthy ones of the country went with them too.

They came to a certain country and they also

Sippurei Maasiyot – Chapter 12

asked the watchmen, "What sort of country is this and who is your king?" They answered them: Inasmuch as when the Storm Wind occurred, then the people of this country chose for themselves that the main purpose is speech. They took up an eloquent talker as a king. Later they found quite a superb, eloquent bard and orator; they accepted him as a king because the king relinquished the kingdom to him because he is so eloquent. They realized, "This must surely be our King's Orator." They also asked if it were possible to be seen by the king. They answered them, "We must announce it." They announced it, and he ordered that they should come in. They entered the king, and that was the King's Orator. They recognized each other, and there was also great rejoicing and weeping between them. The Orator also went with them as well and they went further in search; maybe they would find the rest of them, for they saw that Hashem Blessed his name, is helping them; that they successively find their friends. And they attributed all this to the merit of their kosher Prayer Leader who is always praying for this, and through his prayers, they were privileged to always find their friends. They went onward; maybe they will find the rest in addition.

They went along and they came to a certain country, and they also asked, "What sort of country is this, and who is your king?" They answered that they are of the faction that had chosen for itself that the main goal is to go

Sippurei Maasiyot – Chapter 12

drunk and be happy. They had taken up for themselves some drunkard as a king because he is always happy, but later they found a man sitting in a sea of wine and he pleased them very much more, because this is certainly a very big drunkard, for he's seated in a sea of wine. They took him up as a king. They also asked to interview him and the guards went and announced it. They entered to the king, and this was the King's Faithful Friend who had been sitting in the sea of wine that had come about from the talk of the Orator who consoles them, as mentioned. And the countrymen reasoned that he is a great drunk since he sits in a sea of wine, so they took him up as a king. When they entered to him, they recognized each other, and between them was great rejoicing and weeping, as before. And the Faithful Friend went with them as well.

They went onward and came to a certain country. They asked the watchmen, "Who is your king?" They answered that their king is a beautiful woman, insofar as she leads to the goal because the goal is the habitation of the world that is, that the world should be inhabited with people, as mentioned. And initially, they had a beautiful woman like a queen; then they found a beauty who is a very exceptional beauty and they accepted her as a queen. They realized: this must surely be the Queen's Daughter. They also asked to interview with her, and they went and announced, and they entered to the queen and recognized that this is

Sippurei Maasiyot – Chapter 12

the Queen's Daughter herself. And the rejoicing that was there is certainly unimaginable. They asked, "How have you come here"?

She told them that after the Storm Wind happened and had snatched away the dear boy-Child out of the crib as mentioned, immediately in that frantic moment she ran after the child but did not find him. The milk pressured her and from this, the sea of milk came about. Then the country found her and accepted her as king over them. And there was a great celebration there. But they also wept severely over the dear boy-Child who's not there, and over her father and mother whom she, the Queen's Daughter, doesn't know about. But now already the country has a king too, because already here is the husband of the Queen's Daughter who has become queen here - for the Warrior himself is her man - so now the country has a king!

The Queen's Daughter asked the Prayer Leader for the time being to go in her country and meanwhile cleanse of their repulsive vice because since for them the main purpose was a beautiful woman, they were certainly very defiled and deep in this lust, therefore she asked the Prayer Leader to meanwhile go cleanse them of it a little in the meantime that is, he should tell them **Mussar** [exhortation] so that they should not be so deep in this craving of promiscuity so that they should not be so crude in this vice, because beyond it is a

Sippurei Maasiyot – Chapter 12

craving, it was additionally for them just like a creed that this is the goal because all the factions that had each chosen its bad thing as the purpose, as mentioned - for each of them the thing was just as a creed that this is the purpose, therefore she asked the Prayer Leader to go and cleanse them a little in the meantime. **Then** they all went searching for the rest. They went along and they came to a certain country, and they also inquired, "Who is your king?" They answered them that their king is a one-year-old, for they are from the faction that had chosen for themselves that whoever has an abundance of food and is not nourished from what other people eat - he deserves to be a king. They temporarily accepted a wealthy man as king. Then they found a man who was sitting in a sea of milk, and they were very pleased by him, because this man was nourished his whole life from milk and was not nourished from what other people eat, therefore they took him up as a king. And for that reason, he is called a **Ben Shanah** [one-year-old] since he lives on milk like a one-year-old. They realized that this is surely their Child. They requested to interview with him, and they went and announced. They entered to him and they recognized each other, for he also recognized them, even though he was only a little child when he was snatched away - nevertheless because he was a mature sage since his birth, since he was born with complete wisdom, as mentioned, therefore he recognized them; and

Sippurei Maasiyot – Chapter 12

they, of course, recognized him. There was certainly a very great celebration there, albeit they still wept that they did not know of the King and the Queen. And they asked him, "How did you get here"?

He told them that when the Storm Wind had snatched him away, it carried him away from where it carried him and he was there in that place and sustained himself with what he found there until he came to the sea of milk. He understood that this sea was certainly made from his mother's milk, for the milk certainly pressured her, and that is how the sea came about. He settled there on the sea of milk and was nourished by the milk until these countrymen came and took him up as a king.

Then they went onward and came to a country. And they asked, "Who is your king?" And they replied that they had chosen for themselves that murder is the goal. They accepted a certain murderer as king, then they found a woman sitting in a sea of blood, so they took her up as a king because they saw that she is surely a very great murderer since she is seated in an ocean of blood. They also asked to interview her, and they went and announced. They entered to her, and this was the aforementioned Queen who keeps crying constantly and her tears come to be the sea of blood as mentioned. They recognized each other, and there was certainly a very great celebration there, albeit they still wept that they still did not know about the King.

Sippurei Maasiyot – Chapter 12

They went onward and came to a certain country. They asked, "Who is your king?" They replied that they had chosen for themselves as a king a certain honorable person that is, a person who has honor, as mentioned because for them the main purpose is an honor. Then they found sitting in a field an old man wearing a crown on his head. They were extremely pleased by him, for he is a dignitary, for he sits in a field adorned with a crown, and they accepted him as king. They realized that this is certainly their King himself, and they also asked if it were possible to be seen by him. They went and announced, and they entered to him and recognized that he is the King himself. And the rejoicing that was there is certainly inconceivable in the brain. And the foolish **gods** that is, the very wealthy ones from the land of riches who went with them are traveling with them, and they do not know whatsoever for their lives what is happening here, why there is such happiness here.

And now the entire holy group was restored and gathered together united: that is, the King and the holy people. They sent the Prayer Leader to all the countries that are, the countries of all the factions that had each chosen for itself a bad thing as a goal, as mentioned to correct them and cleanse them; to lead them out of their error, each country out of its vice and its nonsense, for they had all become deluded, as mentioned, and now the Prayer Leader definitely had the power to go to

Sippurei Maasiyot – Chapter 12

them and turn them around to the right way, for he had received power and permission from the kings of all the lands since here where all their kings, as mentioned because the King and his people who had come together - they all were the kings of all the lands of the factions mentioned above. The Prayer Leader went, with their authority, to cleanse them and bring them back in **Teshuvah** [repentance], while the Warrior spoke with the King regarding the country that is so fallen in the gods of money. The Warrior said to the King, "I heard from you that through the way that I have to the Sword - through it, it is possible to extract someone who has fallen in the gods of money".

The King answered him, "Yes, it is so." The King told the Warrior the thing, just how thorough that way one can take them out of the craving of money: Inasmuch as on the way where he goes to the Sword there is a way on the side; by this way, one comes to a Fiery Mountain, and on this Mountain crouches a Lion. And the Lion, when he needs to eat, goes and falls on the flocks and takes for himself sheep and cattle and eats them up. And the shepherds know of this and guard the sheep intensely from him, yet the Lion does not look at this whatsoever - just whenever he wants to eat, he falls on the flocks, and the shepherds bang and strike and storm at him, however, the Lion does not hear this at all; he just takes sheep and cattle for himself and roars and eats them. And the Mountain of Fire is entirely

Sippurei Maasiyot – Chapter 12

invisible in other words, there, there is a Mountain of Fire, only, one doesn't see it.

And moreover, from the side, there is yet another way; with this way, one comes to a place called **Kech** [Kitchen]. And therein that Kitchen there are all sorts of food, and in the Kitchen, there is no fire whatsoever; rather, the foods are cooked by way of the Fiery Mountain mentioned above. And the Fiery Mountain is very far from there, but channels and pipes go from the Fiery Mountain to the Kitchen, and thereby all the foods are cooked. And the Kitchen to is not seen at all, but there is a sign: standing there are Birds upon the Kitchen, and by them, one knows that the Kitchen is there. And the Birds hover with their wings, and thereby they kindle the fire and put out the fire, that is, by the Birds flapping, they blow on and inflame the fire, and also by their very flapping they put out the fire so that the fire should not flame too strongly, more than necessary. And they blow on the fire according to what is necessary for the foods, that is, for one food is needed such a fire, and for another food is needed a different fire - all according to the food, so do the Birds blow on the fire. All this the King tells the Warrior.

Therefore, lead them that is, these people from the Land of Riches who are **gods** there first against the wind, so that the smell of the foods should get to them. Then when you give them from the foods, they will definitely just cast away the craving of money".

Sippurei Maasiyot – Chapter 12

The Warrior did so and took these people, that is, the magnates from the Land of Riches who are gods in their country, who came here with the Warden, as mentioned. Now, when they left their country with the Treasurer, the countrymen gave them power that whatever they do shall be done and the whole country must abide by whatever they do. The Warrior took the people and led them on the way which the King told him, as mentioned and he brought them up until the Kitchen where the foods are. And first, he led them against the wind and the smell of the foods went to them and they began begging him intensely to give them from these good foods. Then he led them away from the wind and they began to scream, "There is a tremendous stench!" He again brought them against the wind and again the good smell of the foods reached them and again they begged intensely that he should give them from the foods, then he again led them away from the wind and they again began to scream, it stinks unbelievably [very wildly].

The Warrior responded to them, "Don't you see that there is nothing whatsoever here that should have a bad smell? It must certainly be that you yourselves make the stench, for here there is nothing that should have a bad smell." Then he gave them food. As soon as they ate of these foods, they immediately began to cast away from themselves their money, and each one dug for himself a grave and buried himself in the pit due to the great disgrace, as they were

Sippurei Maasiyot – Chapter 12

intensely ashamed, for they felt that money stinks intensely, which smells like actual feces because they had tasted of the foods. And they scratched their faces and buried themselves and could not lift their faces at all, and each one was ashamed in front of the other because such is a **Segulah** [special power] of the foods, that whoever eats of the foods is very repulsed by money because there in that place money is the greatest disgrace of all disgraces, and when someone wants to say something derogatory about another, throw something out at another he throws out at him, "You have money," for money, there is a huge disgrace, and the more money someone has, the more he is ashamed, therefore they buried themselves out of great disgrace, and each of them was unable to lift his face even in front of the other; even more so in front of the Warrior. And whoever still found with himself some **Dinar or large** [type of money] would rid himself of it immediately and throw it away from himself. Then the Warrior came to them and took them out of their pits that they had dug for themselves there out of disgrace, and he said to them, "Come with me because now you need no longer have any fear of the Warrior, for I myself am the Warrior!" They begged the Warrior to give them the foods, to bring to their country, because they themselves would surely just hate money, however, they wanted the whole country to go out from this money craving.

Sippurei Maasiyot – Chapter 12

The Warrior gave them from these foods and they brought the foods into their country, and as soon as they gave them from these foods they all immediately began to cast away their money and buried themselves in the earth out of disgrace; and the very wealthy and the gods were most ashamed, but even the lesser people who were called "animals" and "birds" by them were also ashamed for having been so little until now in their own eyes because they had no money because now they knew that on the contrary, it's just the reverse: money is the main disgrace. For these foods have such an effect, that whoever eats from the foods is very repulsed by money, for he senses the bad smell of money, just like feces exactly. They all cast away their money and their gold and silver. Then they sent them the Prayer Leader and he gave them **Teshuvoth** [ways to make amends and return to God] and **Tikkunim** [Fixes], and he cleansed them. And the King became king over the entire world, and the entire world returned to God, blessed be He, and they all were involved only in Torah, prayer, **Teshuvah**, and good deeds. Amen, so be His will. Blessed are Hashem for eternity, Amen and Amen.

Sippurei Maasiyot – Chapter 13

Chapter 13

The Seven Beggars

Once there was a King who had an only son. The King wanted to transfer the kingdom to his son during his lifetime, so he threw a grand party which they call a **BAll**. Now, when the King throws a ball there is certainly great merriment, so especially now that he was transferring the kingdom to his son during his lifetime, there was certainly a very great celebration. And there at the ball were all the royal officers and all the dukes and gentry, and people were very merry at the ball. And the country too was enjoying this - the king's transferring his kingdom to his son in his lifetime - for it is a great honorific event for the King. So, a very great celebration took place there, and there were all types of festivities there: song groups, drama groups and so forth, as well as everything useful just for merriment - it was all there at the ball.

And when they had waxed very merry, the King got up and said to his son, "Being that I am a stargazer, I see that you will at some time fall from the kingship. Therefore, see to it that you have no **Sadness**, that is no grief, when you fall from reign; just be happy. And if you will be happy, I will also be happy. Even if you will have sadness, I will still be happy that you are not king, since you are not fit to be king if you

Sippurei Maasiyot – Chapter 13

cannot keep yourself happy. In other words, if you are the kind of man that you cannot keep yourself happy even when you fall from reign then you aren't fit to be any sort of king. But when you will be happy then I will be extraordinarily happy".

The King's son took over the reign very sharply, appointing his own royal officers, and he had dukes, gentry, and soldiers. Now, this son of the King was a clever person and loved wisdom very much, and very great intellectuals accompanied him. And whoever came to him with some sort of wisdom was very esteemed by him, and he would grant them honor and riches for their wisdom. Whatever each one wanted, he gave him: one wanted money - he gave him money; another wanted to honor - he gave him honor; anything for wisdom. And because studying was so important to him, they all took to wisdom, and the entire country was occupied with **Chokhmoth** [philosophies] because this one desired money - in order to get money for it being his motive - and that one desired status and honor. And because all of them were busy only with philosophies, therefore they all forgot there in that country the strategies of war in other words, how to wage a war, for they were all busy exclusively with philosophies, to such a degree that the smallest person in that country was the greatest sage in another country, while their own wise men were utterly wild scholars. And on account of their philosophies, those wise men

Sippurei Maasiyot – Chapter 13

of the country fell into heresy and drew the son of the King too into their heresy. Albeit the simple folk were not harmed and did not become disbelievers, for there was great depth and subtlety in the sages' wisdom, so the common folk were not able to enter into their wisdom, therefore it did not harm them. Only the wise men and the King's son became heretics.

And the King's son, because there was good in him, for he was born with goodness and had good character traits, would frequently remind himself, "Where am I in the world? What am I doing?" etc. and would make a very big groan and sigh deeply over it. He would ponder, "What is this? I should be carried away with such things?! What's going on with me? Where am I in this world?" as he kept sighing intensely. Albeit as soon as he began to use his intellect the heretical philosophy became strong again in him. This happened numerous times, that he would still contemplate where he is in the world, what he is doing, etc. as above, with groaning and sighing - but as soon as he began using his intellect the heretical belief became strong in him again, as above.

And the day came to pass - there was a flight in a certain country - everyone fled, and as they were fleeing, they went through a forest, losing two children there, a male and a female; someone lost a male and someone lost a female. And they were still little children of four or five years and did not have anything to

Sippurei Maasiyot – Chapter 13

eat, and they screamed and cried because they had nothing to eat. Meanwhile, there came up to them a beggar going along with his **Torbes** [sacks], carrying bread in them, and these children started to nudge him and huddle after him. He gave them bread and they ate. He asked them, "Where have you come here from?" They answered him, "We don't know," for they were little children. And he started going away from them and they asked him to take them with him. He said to them, "This I do not want, that you should go with me." Meanwhile, they took a look - the beggar is blind! It was a marvel for them: since he is blind, how does he know how to go? But in truth, this itself is a novelty, that such a question should occur to them, for they were still young children. However, they were clever children; therefore, it was a wonder to them. He blessed them this blind beggar, "You should be as I am; you should be as old as I," and he left them more bread and went away, and the children understood that Hashem Blessed his name, was watching over them and had sent them here a blind beggar to give them food.

Afterward, their bread ran out, and again they started screaming for food. After that it became night and they passed the night there. In the morning they still had nothing to eat so they screamed and cried. Meanwhile again a beggar comes up who is deaf; they started talking to him and he shows them with his hands and says to them, "I don't hear anything whatsoever."

Sippurei Maasiyot – Chapter 13

And this beggar also gave them bread to eat and started going away from them. They also wanted him to take them with him but he did not want to. And he too blessed them, "That you should be as I am!" and also left them bread and went his way.

Later on, their bread also ran out, and again they screamed as above. Again, there came to them a beggar who was tongue-tied that is, he stammered with his mouth. They began to speak with him and he was mumbling his speech so they didn't know what he was saying - but he did know what they were saying - only they did not know what he was saying, because he was stammering. This beggar also gave them bread to eat and also started to go away as before and also blessed them that they should be as he, and he went away, all as before.

Then there came again a beggar who had a crooked neck and it transpired as before. Then there came again a beggar who was **Hoikir** [hunchbacked]. Then there came again a beggar without hands. Then there came a beggar without feet. And each one of them gave them bread and blessed them that they should be like him, just as the other beggars.

Afterward, the bread ran out by them yet again and they started walking toward a settlement until they came away. They went that way until they came to a village. They children went into a house, and they had pity on them and gave them bread. They continued into another house

Sippurei Maasiyot – Chapter 13

and there to they gave them bread, so they kept going around into houses and they saw things are good for them and they are being given bread. The children decided between them that they should always be together, and they made themselves large **Torbes** [sacks] and went around to the houses, and went to all happy occasions, to **Brissim** [rite of circumcision] and to weddings. And they continued, further along, going into cities, to the houses; and went to market fairs, and would sit among the beggars in the same way they sit there on the **Prizbes** [banks of the earth] with a **Teller** [a plate for collecting alms], until these children became famous already among all the beggars, for all of them recognized them and knew of them; that they were the children who had been lost in the forest as mentioned.

One time there was a big fair in a big city, and all the beggars went there, as well as the children too. It came to the mind of the beggars that they should match the children; that they should marry each other. And as soon as they started discussing it, it pleased all of them and they were matched. But how to make them a wedding? They came to the decision, inasmuch as on such and such a day the King would have his **Myenines** [birthday] feast name day, all the beggars would go there, and from what they would request for themselves there, meat and bread, they would make a wedding. And so it was; all the beggars went to the **Myenines** and requested out for themselves bread and meat

Sippurei Maasiyot – Chapter 13

and also collected what was leftover from the banquet, meat, and bread, which is called **kolitch** [big loaves special for celebrations]. And they went ahead and dug out a big trench which could contain a hundred people and covered it with sticks, earth, and trash, and they all went inside and married the children there, setting up a chuppah for them, and they were very, very happy there; and the groom and bride also were extremely happy. Now the groom and bride started recalling the kindnesses Hashem Blessed his name, had done for them when they were in the forest, and started crying and greatly yearning, "How can the first beggar, the blind one, be brought here, who brought us bread in the forest"?

And just as they were longing very much for the blind beggar he immediately calls out and says: I am here. I have come to you for the wedding, and I'm presenting you with a **Derashah** [Oration] **Geshenk** [gifts given to the groom in reward for his pre-chuppah] that you should be old as I. For previously I had blessed you with this, that you should be as old as I; now I present it to you as a completely free gift, **Derashah Geshenk**, that you should live as long as I. You think that I am blind. I am not blind at all, except all the time of the whole world does not come across me as much as an eye blink thus he appears blind, for he doesn't peek into the world whatsoever, for all the entire world's time doesn't come across him whatsoever, even as an eyeblink, therefore no

Sippurei Maasiyot – Chapter 13

sight or any glimpse of the world at all is relevant to him, because I am very old and I am yet entirely **Yanik** [Young] and have not yet begun living at all - but I am still very old. And it is not I alone that say this; on the contrary, I have an approval upon it from the Great Eagle. I will tell you a story. All this the blind beggar is saying.

One time there were people traveling on many ships on the sea. A storm wind came and broke the ships, and the people were saved. The people came to a tower; they went up on it and found there all kinds of food, drink, clothing, and whatever one needs. And all good was there, and all the delights in the world. They spoke up and said that each one should tell an old story - what he remembers from his first memory, that is, what he remembers since his memory began. There were old and young there and they honored the biggest **Zaken** [elder] among them to tell first.

He answered and said, "What shall I tell you? I remember back when they cut the apple off the branch." No one at all knew what he was saying, however, there were wise men there and they said, "Ooh! - that is a totally old story." Then they honored the second **Zaken**, who was younger than the first, that he should tell. The second one replied, "That there is an old story?!" expressing wonder "I remember that story, but I remember back even when the candle was burning." Those who were there replied, "That story there is older yet than the

Sippurei Maasiyot – Chapter 13

first," and it was a marvel to them that the second one is younger than the first, yet remembers an older story than the first. Then they honored the third **Zaken**, that he should tell. The third one, who was younger yet, spoke up saying, "I remember back even when the construction of the fruit was just beginning; when the fruit was just starting to become a fruit. They answered there, "This is an even older story." Then the fourth spoke up, who was even yet younger, "I remember back even when they were bringing the seed so as to plant the fruit".

The fifth answered, who was even yet younger, "I recall even the sages who thought up and brought out the seed." The sixth, who was even yet younger, called out, "I remember even the taste of the fruit before the taste entered into the fruit." The seventh called out, "I recall even the smell of the fruit before the smell entered the fruit. The eighth answered and said, "I remember even the appearance of the fruit before it went up on the fruit.

And I at the time was just an infant, the blind beggar who is telling all this, and I too was there and I announced, "I remember all these stories - plus I remember Absolutely Nothing. They replied, "That is a story completely older than all of them," and it was a great marvel to them that the child remembers more than them all. In the midst of this came a Great Eagle and knocked on the tower and said to them, "Cease being poor! Return to your treasures and use

Sippurei Maasiyot – Chapter 13

your treasures," and he said to them that they should go out from the tower age by age; whoever is oldest should go out first. He took them all out from the tower, removing the babe first, for truthfully, he is, after all, older than all of them, and likewise whoever was younger he brought out first, and the hoariest elder he brought out at the very end, for the one who was younger was in fact older, because the younger he was, the older a story he kept telling, and the most aged elder was younger than all of them.

The Great Eagle replied to them, "I will explain to you all the stories that everyone told. The one who told that he remembers back when they cut the apple off the branch means: he remembers back even when they cropped his navel, even what happened to him immediately as soon as he was born - when they cut his navel cord - even this he remembers; and the second who said that he remembers back even when the candle was burning means: he remembers back even when he was in utero when a candle burns over one's head, for it says in the **Gemara** [Talmud] that when a child is in the mother's womb a candle burns over his head, etc. and he who said that he remembers back even when the fruit began to form, it is that he remembers back even when his body began to take form when the fetus was only beginning to take form; and the one who remembers back when they were bringing the seed to plant the fruit, it means he remembers

Sippurei Maasiyot – Chapter 13

back even when the droplet was being drawn down [during relations]. And he who remembers the sages bringing out the seed means he remembers back even when the droplet was still in the brain, for the brains emit the droplet, and the one who remembers the taste - it is the **Nefesh** [vital lifeforce]; and the smell - it is the **Ruach** [spirit], and the appearance - it is the **Neshamah** [uppermost soul]. And the babe said that he remembers "absolutely nothing" because he is greater than all of them and remembers even what he was prior to **Nefesh**, **Ruach**, and **Neshamah**; thus, he said he recalls absolute nothingness. In other words, he recalls not existing at all; he remembers even what was happening there, which is highest of all." And the Great Eagle said to them, "Return to your ships, which are your bodies which have been broken and will be rebuilt; now return to them," and he blessed them. And to me, the blind beggar [who was a babe then] who is telling all this said the Great Eagle, "You come with me, for you are like me, for you are 'very old and completely young' and haven't at all started to live and are yet nonetheless very old. And I am like that too, for I am very old and still entirely young, etc." It follows I have a testimonial from the Great Eagle that I am very old and completely youthful, etc.

Now I present it to you as a completely free gift, **Derashah Deshenk** [oration], that you should be as old as I. There was a great

Sippurei Maasiyot – Chapter 13

celebration there with great jubilation and they were extremely happy.

On the following day of the seven days of **Mishneh** [drinking of the celebration], the **Chathan-Kallah** [groom-bride] thought back again about the other beggar, who was deaf, who had enlivened them and given them bread. And they were crying and longing, "How can the deaf beggar, who enlivened us, be brought here?" Meanwhile, as they were longing after him, he comes in and says, "I am here!" And he fell upon them, kissed them, and said to them, "Today I present you in a gift that you should be as I am, that you should live as good a life as I do. Because previously I had blessed you with this; today I give you my good life in a full gift, **Derashah Geshenk**. You think that I am deaf. I am not deaf at all, except that the whole world does not matter to me whatever so that I should hear their lacking. For, each and every voice in the world is only about needs, since everybody screams about his deficit, that is, what he hasn't got; and even all the world's celebrations are all exclusively about deficits, as someone rejoices over what he didn't have whereas now he has what he didn't have. But the entire world doesn't come across me at all, that I should hear their deficit, for I live such a good life that it hasn't any lack at all; and I have an attestation about this, that I live a good life, from the Land of Wealth." And his good life was: he ate bread and drank water. He told them.

Sippurei Maasiyot – Chapter 13

Inasmuch as there is a land where there is great wealth - they have enormous fortunes - one time the wealthy people gathered together and each one began boasting of his good life, how he lives such a good life, and each one described the routine of his good life.

I spoke up and said to them, the deaf beggar who is telling all this: I live a better **Good Life** than you, and this is the proof: for if you live the good life, help out that country - for there is a country where they had a garden, and in the garden were fruits having all kinds of tastes in the world and all kinds of smells in the world; there too in the garden were all kinds of shapes of every color and all the **Kvetin** [flowers] in the world; everything was there in the garden. And over the garden was an **Agradnik** [gardener] that is someone who sees to the garden, and the people of the country would live a good life through the garden. The gardener there got lost, so naturally whatever there is in the garden must surely cease to exist since the gardener is no longer there to see to the garden and go about with what needs to be done around the garden. But despite this, they would have been able to live from the garden's aftergrowth, from the regrowth, that is, what grows in a garden by itself from that which falls down.

A cruel and merciless king came over the country and could do nothing against them, so he went and spoiled the country's good life that they had from the garden. It was not that he

Sippurei Maasiyot – Chapter 13

spoiled the garden, rather he left behind in the country three crews of henchmen and commanded them to do what he ordered them. And by doing there what the king ordered them they ruined the taste, for through what they did there they made it that whoever wanted to feel any taste, it would have the taste of rotten carcass. And similarly, they ruined the smell so that all the smells would have the smell of galbanum, and similarly, they destroyed the appearance, for they made it be dark in the eyes just like when it's cloudy. All this did the three crews of workers accomplish in the country by doing there what the king ordered them, as mentioned. Now if you live the good life let me see if you can help out that country. So is the deaf beggar still saying to the Land of Wealth which had bragged that they live the good life, as mentioned. And I say to you: if you won't help them out, it will harm you too that is, the fact that in that country the appearance, taste, and smell were ruined, will reach you too.

The rich men mentioned above got up to go to that country, and I went with them too, and on the way, they lived their good life, each his own, for they had fortunes as mentioned. When they came nigh to the country, there began to spoil also by them the taste and the other things, and they felt in themselves that it had become spoiled with them. I spoke up to them, "Just consider - if now when you have not yet entered the country, the taste, appearance, and smell have already become spoiled for you,

Sippurei Maasiyot – Chapter 13

how will it be when you go in? And all the more so, how can you still help them?" I took my bread and my water and gave them to them. They felt in my bread and water all the tastes, and all the smells, etc., and everything became corrected that had been ruined for them that is, the taste, appearance, and smell .

And the other country, that is, the country where the garden was where the taste, etc. had been ruined, as mentioned, started to look around to repair the country's ruined taste and so forth. They came to a decision: inasmuch as there is a Land of Wealth that very land mentioned above with whom the beggar had spoken, as mentioned, it felt to them that is, it felt to the country where the garden was that their gardener who had become lost through whom they had lived the good life is from the same root as the people of the Land of Riches who also live the good life; therefore, they liked the idea that they should send off to the Land of Wealth - they will surely help them! They did so and sent messengers to the Land of Wealth. The messengers went, and they encountered each other that is, the emissaries came up against the people of that very Land of Riches on the way, for the Land of Wealth themselves wanted to go to them, as mentioned. They asked the messengers, "Where are you going?" They answered, "We are going to the Land of Wealth so that they will help us." They spoke up, "We ourselves are that rich country and we are going to you".

Sippurei Maasiyot – Chapter 13

I spoke up the deaf beggar who is telling all this to them, "Don't you need me? For you cannot go there and help them," as mentioned above because when they only so much as came near the country, they themselves were already affected; all the more so when etc. as mentioned. "Therefore, you stay here and I will go with the emissaries to help them".

I spoke up the deaf beggar who is telling all this to them, "Don't you need me? For you cannot go there and help them," as mentioned above, because when they only so much as came near the country, they themselves were already affected; all the more so when etc. as mentioned. "Therefore, you stay here and I will go with the emissaries to help them".

Later I went further to another city of that country and saw two people fighting with each other on account of some trade transaction. They went to the courthouse to bring suit and the court decided for them: this one is entitled and that one is obligated - and they went out from the court. Afterward, they again bickered with each other, and said that they no longer want this courthouse - they just want another courthouse - and they chose for themselves another courthouse and brought their case before the other courthouse. Afterward one of them again got into an argument with someone else, and again they selected a different courthouse, and so they fought on and on there, this one with that one and that one with this one, always choosing a different court until the

Sippurei Maasiyot – Chapter 13

entire city was filled with courthouses. I took a look and saw that this was due to there being no truth there; now this one tilts the verdict and favors this one in other words he curries favor with him and decides in his favor, and later the other one favors him in other words later the other decides in his favor in return, for they take bribery and they have no truth there.

Afterward, I saw that they are full of adultery, and there are so many illicit relations there that it has already become an altogether permissible thing for them. And I said to them that on account of this, the taste, the smell, and the vision were ruined for them, for the aforementioned cruel king had left them the three aforementioned squads of agents so that they should go and ruin the country. For they went around and spoke lewd speech among them, bringing lewd speech into the country, and through lewd speech, the result was that the taste was ruined, so that all the tastes had the same taste as **Nevelah** [carcass of an animal]. And likewise, they brought bribery into the country, and thereby their vision was ruined and it got dark in their eyes, for so it states - Bribery blinds the eyes of the wise. And similarly, the henchmen brought lechery into the country, and through this, the smell was ruined, for lechery results in ruined smell and look in another place in our words - that lechery blemishes one's smell. Therefore, you should see that you repair the country from these three sins and seek after these people the agents who

Sippurei Maasiyot – Chapter 13

brought the three sins into the country, as mentioned and drive them out. And when you do so and you purge the country from the three sins, I say to you that not only will the taste, vision, and smell be repaired, but that moreover, even the gardener who was lost from you will also be recoverable.

They did so, and they began cleansing the country of the three sins. And they sought out the people the henchmen mentioned above and they would grab someone and ask him, "From where did you come here?" - until they caught the cruel king's agents and drove them out, and they cleaned out the country from the sins. Meanwhile, a noise was made: Maybe the insane one is the gardener after all? For there is an insane man going about who keeps saying that he is the gardener, and everyone holds him to be insane, and stones are thrown at him and he is driven away - but maybe he in fact is the true gardener?! They went out and brought him that is, before these ones who sat and repaired the country; and also, he, namely the deaf beggar who is telling all this, was there. And I said, "Of course, he is the gardener!" That is, the one whom they had previously called insane. Hence, I have a testament from there that I live the good life, for I myself repaired the Land. Now I present you with my good life as a gift.

A big celebration and great blissfulness started up there, and they were extremely happy. The first one had given them **Chayim Arukhim**,

Sippurei Maasiyot – Chapter 13

that is, long life, and the other had given them **Chayim Tovim**, that is a good life. And so, all the beggars came afterward to the wedding and gave them for a wedding-discourse present the same thing that they had previously blessed them, to be like themselves; they now gave this to them in total gift, **Derashah Geshenk** for a wedding-discourse present.

On the third day, the groom and bride again thought back, crying and longing, "How can the third beggar be brought here, who was a **Kaved-Peh** [tongue-tied]?" That is, who stammered with his mouth. Meanwhile in he comes and says, "I am here!" And he fell on them, kissed them, and he too said to them as before: Previously I had blessed you to be like me. Now I give you **Derashah Geshenk**, that you be like me. You think I am speech-impaired. I am not speech-impaired at all, rather: the utterances of the world which are not praises to the Supernal One have no integrity in other words thus he appears like a tongue-tied person who cannot talk, for he has absolutely no wish to speak any worldly speech which is not praise to Hashem Blessed his name; since talk that is not praise to Hashem Blessed his name; has no integrity, thus he stammers in his speech. But in truth, I am not speech-impaired at all. On the contrary, I am an orator and a speaker, that is, one wild novelty of a good talker. And I can say such wildly innovative riddles, poems, and songs that when I begin to speak my riddles, poems, and songs,

Sippurei Maasiyot – Chapter 13

there can be no creature in the world that will not want to hear me in other words there is not a creature in the world that will not want to hear his poems, etc. And contained in them that is, in the riddles and poems that he says are all the wisdoms. And I have a testimony to this from that great man who is called "The Truly Gracious Man". And there is a whole story to this.

For, once upon a time all the wise men sat, and each one boasted of his wisdom. This one boasted that with his wisdom he had invented the production of the Iron, that one boasted that he had invented another type of metal [zinc or lead], another boasted that with his wisdom he had invented the production of silver - this is already more momentous [the ability to make silver is what he had brought out] another boasted that he had invented the ability to make gold, and another boasted that he had invented weapons of war the instruments with which war is conducted, namely guns, cannons and so forth - the technology of making these instruments is what he brought out; yet another boasted he can produce metal wares without those things that they produce these metals from, and another boasted of other wisdoms, for there are numerous things in the world that have been invented through wisdoms, namely saltpeter, gunpowder and the like. So, each one boasted of his wisdom.

Someone there called out, "I am cleverer than you all, for I am wise as the day." No one there

Sippurei Maasiyot – Chapter 13

understood what he was saying, that he is "wise as the day." He replied to them, "Because all your wisdoms can be put together and they will constitute no more than one hour, even though each wisdom is obtained from a different day, according to the creation that came into being on that day. For all of those wisdoms are composites, several things are mixed together and from them, the thing is produced; therefore, each wisdom is taken from the day in which God created the things from which the materials are taken and combined with wisdom to make the thing they want to make: silver, copper and so forth; in spite of this, all of these wisdoms of yours can be put together by wisdom, constituting no more than one hour. But I am wise like an entire day." So, did that final wise man boast? I tongue-tied who is telling all this called out to him, "Like which day?" In other words, "Like which day are you wise?" He the wise one mentioned responded, "This one here the tongue-tied is wiser than me for he's asking like which day. But like whatever day you wish, that's how wise I am." However, why, after all, is the smarter for having asked like which day, if the wise man himself is also as smart as any day he wishes? But there is a whole story.

For, the Truly Gracious Man is in truth a very great man. And I the speech-impaired who is telling all this go about, gathering up all true generosities, and bring them to the Truly Gracious Man. And the root of time's genesis

Sippurei Maasiyot – Chapter 13

that such a thing as time should exist, for time itself, that is, the very existence of years and days in the world is itself also created by Hashem Blessed his name; is solely through true kindnesses. And I go about and gather up all true kindnesses and bring them to the Truly Gracious Man, resulting in time coming into being.

And there is a Mountain, and on the Mountain stands a stone, and from the Stone emerges a Spring. Now, everything has a heart, and the entire world also has a heart, and the Heart of the World is a complete structure, with face, hands, feet, etc. But the nail of the foot of the World's Heart is **Hertziker** [heartier] than the heart of anything else. And the Mountain with the Stone and the Spring stands at one end of the world, while this Heart of the World stands at another end of the world, and the Heart stands facing the Spring, desiring and hoping continuously, exceedingly, that it should come to the Spring, and the longing and desire of the Heart to come to the Spring is just extraordinary. It screams nonstop, the Heart, to come to the Source, and the Source longs for the Heart too.

Now, the Heart has two things that make it weak. One, because the sun pursues it exceedingly and scorches it is because it always yearns and desires to come to the Source, and the second thing that tires the Heart is due to yearning and desiring, that the Heart constantly yearns and wishes; it keeps pouring

Sippurei Maasiyot – Chapter 13

out its soul for the Source and screaming and so forth, as above, so as to come to the Source, for the Heart is always standing facing the Source, and screams **Na! Gevald!** [Please Woe!], and keeps on yearning most exceedingly for the Source, as mentioned.

However, when the Heart needs to rest a bit, so as to draw a **Zoyfn** [little breath] then comes a Big Bird and spreads its wings above it, shielding it from the sun; then the Heart gets a little rest. But even then, while resting it also looks facing the Spring and still longs for it. But since it longs so much for the Source, why does it not go to the Source? Only, as soon as the Heart wants to go close to the Mountain upon which is the Source then it no longer sees the peak; it cannot look at the Spring - and as soon as it would not look at the Spring it would expire, for the Heart's entire vitality is only from the Source, so when it stands facing the Mountain then it sees the Mountain peak where the Spring is, but immediately as soon as it wants to go to the Mountain, the peak no longer appears for such indeed is the way with a tall mountain; standing from afar the peak is visible, but upon going nearer the peak is no longer visible. Then it can no longer look at the Source and could - Mercy saves us! - expire, and if this Heart - Mercy saves us! - would expire the whole world would be destroyed, for the Heart is the very vitality of everything, and how can the world endure without the Heart? Therefore, the Heart cannot go to the Spring; it

Sippurei Maasiyot – Chapter 13

only stands facing the Spring, longing and screaming without ceasing to be able to come to it, as mentioned.

And the Spring is completely timeless, for the Spring is not within time at all in other words the Spring has no time at all, that is because it is completely above worldly time. So how can Spring exist in the world? For in the world nothing can exist without a time. But all the Spring's time is simply the Heart giving the Spring a day as a gift. And when it comes time for the day to be let out and terminated - and should the day go away, the Source would no longer have any time and would depart from the world — then when the Source is no longer, the Heart itself would also expire, Mercy saves us, then the whole world would become nil, Mercy saves us, as mentioned. Thus, when it gets very close to the end of the day then they begin to take leave of each other which is called **Gizeginin** [wishes and blessings upon departing] - the Heart and the Source - and begin saying wonderful riddles, poems, and songs to one another - very fine riddles and songs - with great love and tremendous yearning one for the other, the Heart for the Source and the Source for the Heart.

Now, the Truly Gracious Man supervises and keeps watch over this, and when the day reaches its very end and needs only to give out at which very instant when the day lets out and the Source shall no longer have any day, as mentioned, it will pass away and thus, Mercy save us, the Heart will expire too; the whole world will be destroyed - at that moment the Truly Gracious Man arrives and gives the Heart a day and the Heart gives the day to the Source; thus the Spring once again has time that day the Source can again maintain its existence and consequently the Heart too can maintain its existence, etc. And when this day comes from the place whence it comes, it comes along with riddles too and with fine poetry which contains all wisdoms. And there are distinctions between the days, for there is a Sunday, a Monday, etc., and similarly, there is a first of the month and holidays in other words, according to what sort of day comes along, with such poetry does it arrive.

And all the time that the Truly Gracious Man has is entirely through me through the tongue-tied one who is telling all this. For I go along and gather up all true generosities, from which all the time comes to exist, as mentioned. And therefore, the tongue-tied one is even smarter than the sage who boasted he is wise like any day one wishes, for time itself and its days altogether come to exist entirely through him, the days coming along with poetry and riddles containing all wisdoms, etc., as mentioned. Hence, I have a testimony from the Truly Gracious Man that I can say riddles and poetry containing all the sciences because all the days, with the riddles and their poetry, come to exist entirely through him, as mentioned. Today I present you in a full gift, **Derashah Geshenk**,

Sippurei Maasiyot – Chapter 13

that you should be like me. There was a grand celebration and superb gladness there, and they had **Zei haben a Hilva gitan** [a ball]

When they had completed that day's celebration and passed the night afterward, in the morning they again thought back and yearned, and so forth, for the beggar who had a crooked neck. Meanwhile in he comes and says: I am here! and so forth... Previously I had blessed you to be like me. Today I present it to you, **Derashah Geshenk**, that you should be like me. You think I have a crooked neck. I have no crooked neck whatsoever. On the contrary, I have a very even neck, a very beautiful neck, except there are **Havalim** [vapors] of the world that is, worldly nonsense, and I wish to release no breath or **Duch** [spirit] whatsoever into the world's vanities, and therefore it appears his neck is crooked since he twists his neck from the world's vanities world and wants to release no breath or spirit whatsoever into the world's vanities. But in truth, I have a very beautiful neck, an extremely fine neck. For I have a superb voice, and all kinds of **Qolot** [sounds] in the world, which are only sound without speech - I can mimic all of them with my voice, for I have a very superb neck and voice. And I have a testament to this from that country.

For there is a country where they are all experts in the science of music-making, and they are all involved there in this wisdom, even little children. There is not a child there who cannot

Sippurei Maasiyot – Chapter 13

play some musical instrument. And the most minor person that is in that country is the greatest expert in another country in musical knowledge. And the sages and king of that country, and the **Cappellas** [song groups], are extraordinarily great masters of that wisdom.

One time the country's sages were sitting together and each one boasted of his **Chokhmah** [musical prowess]. This one boasted he could play on this musical instrument, that one boasted he could play that musical instrument, and another boasted: on another musical instrument. Someone else boasted he could play several musical instruments, and another boasted he could play on all kinds of musical instruments. This one boasted he could perform with his voice like a certain musical instrument, that one boasted he could perform with his voice like a certain musical instrument, and another boasted he could perform with his voice like several musical instruments. Still, another boasted he could perform with his voice exactly like a which is called **Poyk** [drum] when it is struck, and another boasted he could perform with his voice like shooting from **Urmatis** [cannons]. And I too was there the one with the crooked neck who is telling all this. I spoke up and said to them: My voice is better than your voices and this is the proof. because if you are indeed such experts in musical sound, help the two lands.

Sippurei Maasiyot – Chapter 13

For there are two lands, a thousand miles apart from each other. And therein these two countries when night arrives no one can sleep, for when it becomes a night, they all begin crying out with wailing voices - men, women, and children. If a stone were to rest there it would meltdown, for at night they hear an exceedingly wailing sound, and because of it, all of them there must start wailing - men, women, and little children, etc. And this happens in both countries, for in one country they hear the wailing sound and must all lament as have mentioned, and likewise in the other land it too is so, and the two countries are a thousand miles apart. So, if you are such expert musicians, you can play and sing, let me see if you can help the two countries, or at least reproduce the sounds that are, mimic the wailing sound that is heard there. They said to him, "Will you take us there?" He said, "Yes, I take you there [present tense]," and they arose to all go there.

They went and arrived there, at one of the two aforementioned countries. When night came, it was as always - they all began wailing, and the experts too wailed as well. So, they saw for sure they could not help the countries. He said to them that is, the one whose neck was crooked said to the aforementioned sages, "Anyway, tell me where this comes from, that they hear this wailing sound. Where is the sound from?" They said to him, "And do you know?" He replied, "I know indeed".

Sippurei Maasiyot – Chapter 13

For, there are two birds, one male, and one female, and they are just one pair in the world. The female got lost. He seeks her and she seeks him. They had sought each other very long until they lost their ways and saw they can no longer find each other, so they stood still and made themselves nests. He made him a nest nearby one of the two countries - and not actually near it, except that in consideration of the bird's voice it is called near, since from the place where he stopped and made him a nest, they can already hear his voice in that country. And likewise, she also made her a nest near the second country that is, likewise, not right nearby, except there her voice could be heard over there. And when night comes then this pair of birds begin both wailing, for he bemoans her and she bemoans him, wailing with a very big yell. And this is the wailing sound heard in these two countries, because of which they must all begin wailing intensely there and they cannot sleep." So did the crooked-neck continue telling. But they would not believe this, and said to him, "Will you lead us there that is, to the birds"?

He said, "Yes, I can lead you there. Except how can you come there? For if even here you cannot bear the sound and must all wail - when you will come there you will surely be unable to stand it at all! And by day one cannot stand the joy there, for by day the birds gather together by each of them separately, that is, to him and to her, and console them and make

Sippurei Maasiyot – Chapter 13

them happy with extremely great joys, and they tell them words of consolation: "You will still find each other," making them very happy, so much so that by day it is impossible to bear the joy there. And the sound of the birds making them happy is not heard from afar, but only when one arrives there. But the sound of the pair wailing at night - it is heard far away; you cannot, therefore, come there." They said to him, "Can you correct this"?

He replied, "Yes, I can correct it. For I can mimic all the world's sounds that is, all kinds of sounds in the world, he can emit them with his voice, making it exactly like any sound at all; furthermore, I can throw voices, that is, I can throw a sound which here, in the place where I let it out, will not be heard at all - only somewhere far away will it be heard - and therefore I can throw her voice to him, that is, the sound which I will let out will arrive close to the place where he is, and likewise I can throw his voice so that it arrives close to her; thereby will I draw them together" until he brings them together. But who would believe this?

He went and led them into a forest. They heard as if someone opens a door, shuts it again, and slams the bolt **Klaymke** [shut]; and firing from **Biks** [gun], sending the dog to fetch the thing that he was shooting, and the dog thrashing in the **Gigraznit in Shney** [snow]. The sages heard all this, and they looked around - they saw nothing at all, and also from him they

Sippurei Maasiyot – Chapter 13

heard nothing at all. It could only be that he, the crooked neck, was throwing those sounds. So, they saw for sure that he can replicate all kinds of sounds exactly, and also throw sounds. And he did not talk more about this but went up afterward. Hence, I have testament from that country that I have a wonderfully fine voice and I can replicate all the world's sounds. Today I present this to you completely in a gift, **Derashah Geshenk**, to be like me. There was a grand celebration there and extremely high spirits.

On the fifth day, they were also happy. They remembered the beggar who was a **hoikir** [hunchback], and they yearned very much, "How can that hunchback beggar be taken here? For if he were here, the joy would be immense." In the midst of this, he arrives and says, "I am here! I have come to you for the wedding." And he fell on them, hugged them and kissed them, and said to them:

On the fifth day, they were also happy. They remembered the beggar who was a **Hoikir** [hunchback], and they yearned very much, "How can that hunchback beggar be taken here? For if he were here, the joy would be immense." In the midst of this he arrives and says, "I am here! I have come to you for the wedding." And he fell on them, hugged them and kissed them, and said to them

Previously I had blessed you that you be like me; today I present you, **Derashah Geshenk**, that you should be like me. And I am not

Sippurei Maasiyot – Chapter 13

Hoikir [hunchback] whatsoever. On the contrary, I have the **Pleytses** [sort of shoulders] that are the little that holds the much. And I have a testament to this.

For, there was once a conversation in which people boasted about this matter, each one boasting that he has this feature of the little holding the much, in other words, a small space containing very much. They laughed and scoffed at one of them, and the rest who boasted about this feature of the little holding the much were accepted. But my little that holds the much is greater than all of them.

For, one of them boasted that his brain is a "little that holds the much," for he carries in his brain thousands and myriads of people with all their needs, all their customs, and all their discussions and movements. He carries all this entirely in his brain, so he is a little that holds the much since a bit of his brain bears on it so many people with their needs and so forth. Therefore, he is called a little that holds the much, that is, a bit of space containing and bearing so much, namely the bit of brain bearing so many people with all their affairs, etc. They laughed him off and those present there replied, "You are nothing and your people are nothing".

One of them spoke up and said, "I have seen such a little that holds the much. For, once I was passing by before a mountain and I saw a huge amount of garbage and filth on it. It was a novelty for me - from where does so much garbage and filth come on the mountain? There was a man thereby that mountain. The man said It's all mine. For he was dwelling there beside the mountain, and kept throwing on the mountain his garbage and secretions from his eating and drinking, and defecated there until there was so much garbage and feces from him on the mountain. So, this man is a little that holds the much, insofar as so much garbage comes about from one man. That's what this is too." That is, so is the little-that-holds-the-much of the one who boasted that his brain bears so many people, etc.

One of them said inasmuch as he has a **Pardes** [orchard] namely, a garden - a very fine one, where there are fruits and so forth: A great many people and noblemen travel there, for it is quite a nice orchard. And when summer comes, very many people and noblemen travel there to take walks there, and in truth, there is in no way to be found in the orchard so much space as to contain that many people. This, then, is a little that holds the much. His words also pleased them.

One of them said that his speech is a little that holds the much, for he is a private secretary for a great king, and to the king, very many people come. One comes with praises to the king, each one says praise to the king, another comes with petitions for the king, and so forth; and the king certainly cannot hear out all of this. "I gather up all their words into just a few words and tell the king just these few words. Contained in

Sippurei Maasiyot – Chapter 13

them are all their praises and petitions, with all their words entering into my few words which I tell the king. Therefore, my speech is a little holding the much".

One of them said that his keeping silent is a little that holds the much, for he has against him very many accusers and slanderers who gossip very much about him, for they argue with him and talk about him very much. And to whatever they slander him, bicker with him, and accuse him with much gossip, he performs some silence, and that is the solution to all the questions and all the utterances spoken against him. Hence his silence is a little holding the much.

One of them said that he is a little that holds the much, for there is a poor person who is **Well-Visioned** [that is, blind] and very large, whereas he that is, the one who was boasting and telling this is very small and leads about the large poor one who is blind. Hence, he is a little holding the much, for the blind one could slip and fall, but he holds him up with his guidance, and due to this he is a little that holds the much since he is a small person and holds the big blind one.

And I hunchback who was telling all this was also there. I declared: It is true that you have the feature of the little that holds the much. And I know what all of you meant that is, all those who boasted one by one of their little that holds the much - he knows what each of them meant; even the final one who boasted that he leads around the big blind one. He is greater than all of you. But I am still greater and higher than all of you. For, he who boasted that he walks the big blind one, his meaning is that he conducts the lunar **Cycle** [heavenly orb where the moon is], for the moon is called **blind**, for she does not shine in-and-of herself, and she has nothing of her own whatsoever **Veleith Lah Migarmah Klum** [whatsoever], and he who boasted in this conducts the moon, even though he is small and the moon is very great; and this gives the entire world sustenance in other words, by means of this the entire world has existence, for the world needs the moon. Hence, he is definitely a little that holds the much, for sure. However, all the same, my little that holds the much is completely higher than all of them. And here is the proof.

For, once there was a group that investigated: Inasmuch as every beast has its shade its shadow in which it specifically wants to rest, and conversely there is a special shadow for each animal because each and every beast chooses for itself some shadow, and only in that shadow specifically does it want to rest; similarly, each bird has its branch on which it specifically wants to rest, and not on any other branch, while another bird has its own branch and only there can it rest and not on any other; and so each and every bird has its own special branch - therefore the group investigated if there could be found such a tree in whose shadow all the beasts could rest, in that all the

Sippurei Maasiyot – Chapter 13

beasts would want to dwell in the shadow of that tree, and upon whose branches all the birds of the sky would rest. And they discovered that there is such a tree. They wanted to go there to that tree, for the delight that there is thereby that tree is absolutely limitless, since all the birds and all the beasts are found there, and there is no harm whatsoever from any animal, that is to say, no beast injures anyone there, and all the animals there are freely mixed. They all engage in play there and it is certainly a very wonderful pleasure to be there at that tree. They began to examine rationally which **Tzad** [side] they needed to go to come to that tree, and there fell a dispute between them regarding this, without there being anyone among them to decide, for one said that they needed to go to this site to the east, and another said to the west side they needed to go; one said here, another said there, and so on, until they could not discern the right side to go to in order to come to that tree.

A sage came along and said to them, "Why are you investigating by which side to go to the tree? Find out first who are the people who can come to the tree! Because to that tree, not every man can come, since no one can come to the tree except one who has the tree's **Midoth** [attributes]. For, this tree has three roots: One root is faith that one should believe in God, blessed be He, the other in awe, and the third is humility, that is, to not have a special regard for oneself, and the truth is the tree's body, that is,

Sippurei Maasiyot – Chapter 13

the tree itself is truth, and from there go out branches. Therefore no one can come to the tree but one who has these traits of the tree." Faith - he should believe in God; Fear - he should have fear of God, and humility - he should not have any special regard for himself; and truth. So, did the sage say to the group?

The group, however, did not all have these attributes; only some of them had in them these traits. But they had between them very great unity that is, the group all loved each other and held themselves tightly together. They did not want to separate from each other in order that some of them should go to the tree that is, those who already had these traits of the tree and the rest should stay behind - they did not want this, for they held themselves very much together. Instead, they had to wait until the rest of the men would exert themselves in attaining these attributes so that they could all come to the tree.

And so, they did, toiling until they all came to those traits mentioned above. That is, they all waited for each other until each had toiled and they all came to those virtues mentioned above, that is, by now they all have faith, fear, and so on, as mentioned. No sooner did they all come to the attributes, when they all came to one mindset and all agreed on one way by which to go to the tree. They all went. They went along for a while until they could see the tree from afar. Meanwhile, they take a look and the tree is standing in no place at all, for the tree has no space whatsoever. And since it has no place

Sippurei Maasiyot – Chapter 13

whatsoever, how can anyone come to it?

And I'm the hunchback was also there with them. I announced to them, "I can bring you to the tree. For the tree has no place whatsoever, for the tree is completely above space in other words, it is higher than worldly space; it has no place whatsoever, and the aspect of the little that holds the much still takes place in space, for although it is a little that holds the much, that is, a little space holding much more than can be put in the space, in any case, it still takes place in space, because after all it still occupies some sort of space in any case. But I the hunchback have such a little that holds the much that it is the absolute edge of the place beyond which there is no space whatsoever. Therefore, I can carry you all to the tree, which is above space completely. For, this hunchback is something like an intermediary, that is, a midpoint, between space and above space, for he is the ultimate degree of the little holding the much, which is the actual end of space, above which there is no unit of space whatsoever, since from there and above is the aspect of completely beyond space. Therefore, he can take them out of space and bring them above space. Understand this. I took them and carried them to the tree. Hence, I have a testament that I have such an ultimate degree of the little holding the much. And that is why he appeared as a hunchbacked person, for he carries a great deal on him, for he is a little holding the much. Today I give you this very thing is a gift, that

Sippurei Maasiyot – Chapter 13

you should be like me. A great joy took place there, and a superb gladness.

On the sixth day, they also rejoiced, but they also yearned, "How can the one without hands be brought here?" Meanwhile in he comes and says, "I am here! I have come to you for the wedding." And he too spoke to them as the others, falling on them, kissing them and saying to them: You think I am crippled in the hands. I am not at all crippled in the hands. I do have power in the hands, only I do not use the power in my hands in this world, for I need the power for something else - and regarding this, I have a testament from the **Fun Das Vasirikn Shloss** [Watery Castle].

For, once several of us were sitting together. Each one was boasting of the power he has in his hands. This one boasted he has such a strength in his hands, that one boasted he has such a strength in his hands, and so each one boasted of his strength he has in his hands. Namely, one was boasting that he has such a power and a strength in his hands, that when he shoots an arrow he can pull it back to him again, for he has such a power in his hands, that although he has already shot the arrow, he can yet turn it around and tow it back to him again.

I asked him, "What kind of arrow can you pull back?" For there are ten kinds of arrows since there are ten kinds of poison. For, when one wants to shoot an arrow, one smears it with poison. There are ten kinds of poison, and when they soak it in one poison, it injures like so, and when they soak it in another poison it does more damage. And so, there are ten kinds of poison, each one worse than the other, that is, more harmful. And this in itself is ten kinds of arrows, for the arrows are one sort; it is only because of the variety of the poisons that they smear the arrows in, which are ten kinds as mentioned above, that they are called ten kinds of arrows.

So, he asked him, "What kind of arrow can you pull back?" In addition, he asked him whether [only] before the arrow has struck someone, he can pull it back, or whether even after the arrow has already struck someone, he could also pull it back. Upon this, the other answered: "Even after the arrow has already struck someone, I can still pull it back." "But still, which sort of arrow can you pull back?" He answered: Why this-and-this kind I can pull back.

I the one without hands who is telling all this, called out to him, "You cannot heal the Queen's Daughter. If you can pull back no more than one kind of arrow, you cannot heal the Queen's Daughter".

One was boasting that he has such a power in his hands that whoever he receives from, he gives to, by his very getting something from someone, he gives to that person, and hence he is a master of charity. I asked him, "What kind of charity do you give?" For there are ten kinds of charity. He replied: he gives tithe. I called out to him, "If so, you cannot heal the Queen's Daughter, for you cannot at all come to her

Sippurei Maasiyot – Chapter 13

place, because you only give a tithe, for you can enter in no more than one wall in the place where she is dwelling, therefore you cannot come to her place".

One boasted that he has the following power in his hands: "Inasmuch as there are officials in the world senior men who are encharged with giving orders over a city, a country, etc. each one needing wisdom: I have such a power in my hands, that with my hands I can give him wisdom, by laying my hands on him." I asked him, "What kind of wisdom can you give with your hands?" For there are ten **Kabin** [measures] of wisdom, that is ten varieties of knowledge. He replied: Such-and-such wisdom I can give. I called out to him, "If so, you cannot heal the Queen's Daughter, for you cannot even know her pulse, because there are ten varieties of pulses, and you cannot know but one pulse, since you can only give one wisdom with your hands".

One boasted that he has such a power in his hands: when there is a **Ruach Se'arah** [tempest spirit] that is, a storm wind he can detain the storm wind with his hands. He can seize the storm wind with his hands, restraining it, and can moreover with his hands make the wind with a mass, that it should be the sort of wind that is needed; with the proper weight.

I asked him, "What kind of wind can you grasp with your hands?" There are ten varieties of winds. He replied: Such-and-such a wind. I called out, "You cannot heal the Queen's

Sippurei Maasiyot – Chapter 13

Daughter, for you cannot at all play the melody for her. For there are ten varieties of melody, and the Queen's Daughter's healing is through melody, and you can play for her no more than one melody".

They called out, "What can you do?" He replied, "I can do what you all cannot do, namely, all the nine parts of each thing that each one boasted of, which you cannot do, I can do. For, there is a story.

For, one time a king desired cooked himself up about a Queen's Daughter, involving himself with executing schemes to capture her, until the thing was attained and he caught her; then she was with him. One time the king dreamed that the Queen's Daughter stood over him and killed him. He awoke sharply [caught himself up], and the dream entered deep in his heart. He called all the dream interpreters and they interpreted it for him according to its simple meaning, that the dream would be fulfilled according to its simple meaning, that she would kill him. The king could not give himself any counsel, what to do with her. To kill her - would pain him; to send her away from him - this vexed him severely, for another man would take her, and this vexed him very much, for he had made so much effort for her, and now she would come to another man's hand, and moreover, if he let her go and she came to another man's hand, then certainly the dream could be fulfilled that she would kill him since she was by another. To hold her fast by him -

Sippurei Maasiyot – Chapter 13

he feared because of the dream, lest she kills him. So, the king did not know what to do to her. Meanwhile, his love for her perished little by little because of the dream, he no longer loved her so much as before, and at each moment the love perished more and more, and likewise, by her, the love perished more each moment, until it became by her a hatred of him. She fled from him.

The king sent after her to seek her, and they came and told him that she was circling around the Watery Castle. For there is a Watery Castle, and there are ten walls there, one inside the other, and all ten walls are complete of water, and also the ground in the Castle that they walk on is also of water. And likewise, the garden, with its trees and their fruits, are entire of water. As for the beauty of the Castle and the novelty of this Castle, there is no need to talk, for it is certainly a very wonderful novelty, for the whole Castle is of water. Entering the Castle is certainly impossible, for one would drown, for the whole Castle is entire of water. Now the Queen's Daughter, upon fleeing, reached the Castle and was circling there around the Castle. They told the king that she was circling there around the Castle.

The king and his soldiers went to catch her. When the Queen's Daughter saw this, she decided she would run into the Castle, for she wanted more to drown in water than that the king should catch her and she be with him, and perhaps she would be saved after all and she

Sippurei Maasiyot – Chapter 13

could slip into the Watery Castle. When the king saw, that she was running into the water, he said, "If that is the case, well then..." He ordered to shoot her; if she dies, she dies. They shot her and all the ten types of arrows that are smeared with the ten types of poisons struck her. And she, the Queen's Daughter, ran into the Watery Castle and entered into its interior, passing through all the doors of the watery walls. For there are doors there in the watery walls, so she passed through all the doors of all the ten walls of the Watery Castle, until she entered into the Castle's interior, fell down, and remained faint.

And the handless one who is telling all this heal her. For whoever does not have in his hands all the ten varieties of charities cannot enter past all the ten walls of the Watery Castle, for he would be drowned in water. So, the king and his soldiers pursued after the Queen's Daughter and were all drowned in water. But I can enter past all the ten walls of the Watery Castle.

Now, the walls of water are sea waves standing like a wall. The winds are what erect the waves of the sea and hold the waves up. And these waves, which are what the ten walls are, stand there constantly, but it is the winds that hold the waves and erect the waves. And I can enter past all the ten walls of the Watery Castle, and I can pull out from her that is, from the Queen's Daughter all the ten varieties of arrows.

And I know all the ten varieties of pulsebeats through the ten fingers, for through each finger

Sippurei Maasiyot – Chapter 13

of the ten fingers one can know a particular pulsebeat from the ten varieties of pulsebeats, and I can heal the Queen's Daughter through all the ten varieties of melodies, for her healing is through melodies, as mentioned. Therefore, I do, in fact, heal the Queen's Daughter. Hence, I have such power in my hands. Today I give you this very thing as a gift." There was a grand celebration there, and they were superbly happy .

This story is very hard for me to tell, but because I've already begun telling it, now I have to finish it. But he did not actually finish telling it. In this story, there is not one word that will be void of meaning, and whoever is adept and versed in **Sefarim** [Books] can at least understand some of the hints. And the arrows - of which that character boasted he could pull back arrows, this is found in the verse - If I have twofold My sword like lightning [as lightning flashes from one end of the sky across to the other end, against My people in retribution], My hand will yet have to hold on strict justice..." and as Rash"i explains, "Flesh and blood shoots an arrow and cannot retrieve it, but the Holy One, Blessed be He, shoots an arrow and does have the ability to retrieve it as if He were holding them in His hand." And the charity which safeguards against the walls of water - this is also found in a verse: If you would listen to My commandments then your peace would be as a river, and your **Charity** [righteousness] as the waves of the sea. And the

Sippurei Maasiyot – Chapter 13

wind - his grasping it in his hands - this is found in, who has grasped the wind in his fists?" Which is an aspect of producing melody, as explained elsewhere. And the ten types of pulses and ten kinds of melody - this is already explained in the Zohar. All this we heard explicitly. But who, when, and what? Beyond this he said nothing more, that is to say, who they all are, what this is, and when this all took place - this is unknowable.

The conclusion of the story - that is, what happened on the Seventh Day with the footless beggar, and the conclusion of the King's son with whom the story began - he did not tell; and he said he would not tell any more, and it will not be heard until Mashiach comes - speedily in our days, Amen!

He also said, "If I did not know any other thing besides this story, I would still be wild news." He said so explicitly. For this story is very wild news. Contained herein it is very many moral lessons and much Torah, for it contains many teachings and speaks of many ancient tzaddikim; of King David, peace be upon him, for King David stood at the world's edge and cried out to the Spring that flows from the Rock that is on the Mountain, as mentioned above, as written in Tehilim - From the end of the earth I will cry unto You when my heart is faint. Lead me to the rock that is higher than I".

[**All** this we heard from his mouth explicitly. And what is understood from his words is that King David, peace be upon him, is the aspect

Sippurei Maasiyot – Chapter 13

of the Heart, as has been transmitted, and he is hinted to in the story regarding the Heart of the world, which stands at the end of the earth, facing the Spring, crying and longing for it constantly, etc. But still, the words are closed up; fortunate is whoever will merit attaining secrets of this story].

The matter of King David and the aforementioned scripture, "From the ends of the earth," that is hinted at in the story, pertains to the Third Day because there it speaks about the Heart and the Spring; look there and you will see wonders, how in each matter wonderful things are hinted. In this story are found very, very great secrets of the Torah, from beginning to end. All the stories of this book are thoroughly great secrets of the Torah; each word and each thing mean something completely different - but this story is above them all. And of the greatness of the awesomeness of this story, it is not possible at all to tell, for it is above all of them. Exceedingly **Ashrei Ashrei** [fortunate fortunate] is whoever will merit even in the Coming World to know of it just a little bit. And whoever has a brain in his skull, let the hairs of his flesh stand on end; let him understand a little of the greatness of the Creator, blessed be He, and the greatness of the true Tzaddikim, when he looks well into this awesome story, the likes of which will not be heard.

The matter of the verse, "From the ends of the

Sippurei Maasiyot – Chapter 13

earth," mentioned above, pertaining to the story of the Third Day - this I heard explicitly from his holy and awesome mouth, of blessed memory. Furthermore, look at this which I found afterward - that the majority of the words of the chapter of Tehillim where this verse is written, which is - virtually all of it is explained there in hints of the lofty secrets of the story of the Third Day mentioned above: "You will add days onto the days of the King" etc. - for he always needs that they should add days to his days, etc. as mentioned. Summon mercy and truth, that he may preserve it" - this is the True Man of Kindness, etc. "Der Groyser Man; Der Emesir Ish Chesed" - because all the time and the days are made via the Great Man, who is the True Man of Kindness as mentioned there in the story, and he gives and adds at each moment, days to the days of the king, who is the Heart, which is the concept of King David, peace be upon him, as mentioned. And this is, "that he may preserve it" - because he guards and protects, for as soon as the day comes very close to ending - and then the Spring and the Heart and the entire world would end, God forbid - then the True Man of Kindness protects and guards this, and comes and gives a day to the Heart, etc. as mentioned. And this is, "So will I sing praise unto Your name forever, that I may perform my vows **Yom Yom** [day by day] - because each and every day which He gives him, he comes with songs and poems, etc. as mentioned. "I will trust in the covert of Your

Sippurei Maasiyot – Chapter 13

wings, Selah" - for when the Heart needs to rest, a Great Bird comes and spreads Its wings over it, etc., and this is, "I will trust in the covert of Your wings" etc.

Belongs to the first day, The matter of the elders who boasted each and every one of what he remembers, that it is remembered even when the umbilical cord was cut off, etc., And this was the little old man in all of them, etc. Our Rabbi said our memory is a blessing, that in the Gomera It is of this kind: that Shmuel boasted to himself that he remembers the pain of the word, etc. Look there.

Who can glorify or tell? Who can evaluate? Who can estimate even one minuscule of the millions or billions of **Hitnotzetzoth** [illuminations], a bit of the clues of wonders from the very, very awesome and high secrets of this awesome story, which is full of secrets from beginning to end? One who is enlightened in the matter will find goodness and **Hitnotzetzuth** of certain clues according to his capacity.

Milton Keynes UK
Ingram Content Group UK Ltd.
UKHW022350201024
449848UK00007B/70